sacred life

SPIRITUAL PRACTICES FOR EVERYDAY LIVING

ANCIENT FAITH SERIES

sacred life

SPIRITUAL PRACTICES FOR EVERYDAY LIVING

ANCIENT FAITH SERIES

BAREFOOT
MINISTRIES

Kansas City, Missouri

Copyright 2008
by Barefoot Ministries®

ISBN 978-0-8341-5013-3

Printed in the
United States of America

Editor: Mike Wonch
Assistant Editors: Jason Sivewright and Stephanie Wilson

Cover Design: Brandon Hill

Library of Congress Control Number: 2008923831

10 9 8 7 6 5 4 3 2 1

Contents

Introduction

Have you ever seen old pictures of your parents and noticed how out of style they looked? Whether it was your dad's ties that were so wide (or narrow, depending on how old they are!) or your mom's hair which was so big . . . sometimes it is hard to believe those styles were ever cool. Occasionally in the background of those old photos, if you can see anything behind your mom's big hairdo, was a car. Maybe it was a 1950's Chevy, a 1960's Mustang, or even a 1970's muscle car. Somehow, even now, that car is still cool. Some cars, it seems, just never go out of style (except maybe the Chevy Vega or the American Motor's Gremlin). Those cars become the "classics" that are forever in-style and forever cool. The practices in this book are kind of like those classic cars.

These practices might not be well known or commonly practiced in your local church, but when you encounter deeply spiritual people—those intentionally seeking to grow in Christlikeness—you will often find that these people are quite well-acquainted with the classic practices of the Christian faith.

Something important to understand about these practices, they do not make you super-Christian. It is also true that you are not required to do these things to become more like Jesus Christ (which is the goal of the Christian's life) or gain eternal life. These various prayer practices, in the words of Dallas Willard, *"have no value in themselves."*[1]

You might ask, "If they have no value, then why would we want to read a book about them?" These practices are what a Wesleyan would call a "means of grace." They are a means to an end. That *end*, in this situation, is access to God's "grace" which enables growth toward Christlikeness. In the words of John Wesley (a theologian from the 18th Century and the founder of Methodism), the *"means of grace"* are *"the ordinary channels whereby he* (God) *might convey to men* (and women) . . . *grace."*[2] In other words, these practices put us into a position to receive grace from God, to experi-

---

1. Willard, Dallas. *The Spirit of the Disciplines: Understanding How God Changes Lives* (San Francisco: Harper and Row, 1988), 137.
2. *The Works of John Wesley*, 5:187-88.

ence God's unearned favor toward us, and to move us forward in our pursuit of becoming more like our Savior, Jesus.

These practices, known as spiritual disciplines, are not unlike the workouts that a coach might assign to a person wishing to become better in their respective sport. If a particular athlete desires to grow stronger at a rate faster than they would by simply participating in the team practices, the athlete might ask the coach for other exercises he or she can do on personal time. The coach did not assign them, it was not required for the athlete to take on this additional regime, but this person did so out of his or her desire to become a better athlete. In a similar way, those of us that are "compelled by Christ's love" to become more aligned in His steps might choose to take up these spiritual disciplines as tools to grow in our faith. Practicing these disciplines do not earn us greater favor with God, are not mandatory, and do not make us spiritually superior to those who do not practice them. They are simply some of the many ways we can experience the grace of God—His gift—that enables our growth.

When it comes to workouts, the same routine can get old and mind numbing. In fact, many personal trainers recommend changing a particular workout regime every 4-6 weeks in order to stimulate greater muscle flexibility and growth. As they have found, our bodies can become accustomed to a particular workout schedule—so accustomed, in fact, that the benefit of the exercise can be significantly reduced. In order to maximize our efforts, it is important to modify routines frequently. Similarly, the same can happen in the spiritual dimension of our lives. We can become so accustomed to a particular routine (or lack of one) that the benefit of growth that ought to be characteristic of practicing a spiritual discipline can be considerably reduced. To counter this, *Sacred Life* has included nine different spiritual practices with which you can experiment.

"Experiment" is a good way to look at it, too. Not all of these practices will work for each person. There is a need to customize your own pathway of practicing these spiritual disciplines. Consider approaching each discipline as an "experiment." If one does not connect with you, then try another. In time, you will find two or more that fit well for you.

After that, it is up to you to take time to regularly practice them. They are not called spiritual *disciplines* by accident. It takes discipline to do just about anything worthwhile. The same is true of your spiritual journey. It has been said by many Christian authors that the "Christian life is the disciplined life."

On behalf of all the contributors of this book, I welcome you to this experiment in discipline. It is our corporate hope and prayer that the practices you encounter within this book will permit you to experience God's grace in new and profound ways and propel you forward on your journey toward Christlikeness. Although you may not find each of these practices fit your own personal *style*, be assured that they are all *classics* that have proven their usefulness over the centuries.

Grace and Peace,
Mike Kipp

IGNATIUS EXAMEN

By Mike Kipp

Historical Background

Ignatius was born in 1491 in the Basque country of Spain. He was the last of thirteen children born into nobility and raised in the family castle of Loyola. Ignatius enjoyed the privileged life and reflected its characteristics. He became rather addicted to gambling, dueling, romance, and other worldly lures.[3]

In 1517, at the age of 26, he joined the army. Four years later he found himself defending the fortress in the town of Pamplona against the French. During the battle, a cannonball wounded one of his legs and broke the other.[4] The wounds were serious, and Ignatius was forced to return to his family's home in Loyola. He was required to remain in bed for months. During this time he requested books to read and was given *The Life of Christ*.[5] Upon reading this book, and reflecting on his messy personal life, Ignatius experienced a dramatic conversion. As a result he sold all his worldly possessions, wore only sackcloth, and set out to visit the city of the Lord's birth.

Although his broken leg was set, it did not heal. It was therefore necessary to break it a second time in order to reset it correctly (all done without the benefit of anesthesia). Ignatius was not expected to live. However, in late June he took an unanticipated turn for the better. The broken leg did heal, but was shorter than the other. The rest of his life Ignatius walked with a limp. This limp became a constant reminder of his previous life. Ignatius died in 1556 at the age of 65.[6]

What the brief bio above does not explain is the vital connec-

---

3. Foster, Richard J., and James Bryan Smith, eds. *Devotional Classics: Selected Readings for Individuals and Groups* (San Francisco: Harper, 2005), 193.

4. <http://www.luc.edu/jesuit/ignatius.bio.html>. Accessed November 21, 2007.

5. Foster and Smith, *Devotional Classics: Selected Readings for Individuals and Groups*, 193.

6. <http://www.luc.edu/jesuit/ignatius.bio.html>. Accessed November 21, 2007.

tion (which we will visit shortly) between Ignatius' life as a wealthy and worldly person and the legacy he left us in his writings as a Christian. Undoubtedly the most well-known of his writings is *The Spiritual Exercises*. In *The Exercises*, Ignatius outlines a considerable number of practical approaches to applying Jesus' teaching to our lives. We are specifically going to investigate only one of that large collection of exercises. This one is known as the *General Examen of Conscience*.

This exercise is, as its name indicates, a method to take stock of one's general state and spiritual fitness, or to examine one's conscience. Let's begin by looking at this exercise as Ignatius wrote it:

> ✤ The **first** point is to give thanks to God our Lord for the benefits I have received from Him.
>
> ✤ The **second** is to ask grace to know my sins and rid myself of them.
>
> ✤ The **third** is to ask an account of my soul from the hour of rising to the present examen, hour by hour or period by period; first as to thoughts, then words, then deeds.
>
> ✤ The **fourth** is to ask pardon of God our Lord for my faults.
>
> ✤ The **fifth** is to resolve, with His grace, to amend them. Close with an Our Father.[7]

Although a bit awkward to our contemporary eyes and ears, the general thrust of the *Examen* is not lost. Ignatius instructs us to begin in thanksgiving (as the Apostle Paul instructs us in I Thessalonians 5:18 and elsewhere), move to self-awareness, and then deeper self-awareness. This leads to humility, forgiveness, and to a new resolve to put our sin behind us. The ending instruction of closing with an *"Our Father"* is simply a reference for repeating the prayer that Jesus taught His disciples to pray in Matt. 6:9-15 and Luke 11:1-4. To actually take the intentional steps, and necessary time and space, to do this thoroughly will certainly convict us of one of the many ways each of us falls short of God's ideal way of living—revealed to the world through the life of Jesus Christ. The point of taking this sort of "exam" is to facilitate one's self-awareness of their daily living. The point is not to dwell on one's sin, but to see it as it is—a break in relationship with God and others—and

---

7. Tyson, John R., ed. *Invitation to Christian Spirituality: An Ecumenical Anthology* (New York: Oxford, 1999), 251.

seek to correct it. Only when we take the time to reflect on our daily lives do we slow down enough to recognize things we would have missed otherwise. We may see the good we have done, but more often we "skim over" the things that are not as pleasant to remember. That is the point of the particular attention given to one's sin.

In light of the fact that the first half of life Ignatius was admittedly selfish and pleasure-seeking, it strikes me as quite notable that he could so capably create a very practical and simple method of doing a general examine of one's conscience. It could be interpreted that his close acquaintance with such self-centered thinking (and subsequent behavior) served to compel him to closely scrutinize this area in his life, and to realize it was necessary to do so very regularly. In doing this, he ended up helping others look closely at their own lives and thus avoid the common pitfalls found there. So it seems that the predominantly selfish life that Ignatius led during his first thirty years uniquely prepared him to write *General Examen*. This writing not only helped him to live more in step with Christ, but continues to help all those who take his writing seriously. It is remarkable how God takes the whole of our lives—no matter how sordid—and makes good of them and good come from them![8]

Lost in Translation

After his conversion and pilgrimage to Jerusalem, Ignatius decided to better his education. In the midst of his studies, his leadership qualities and deep passion for following Christ won him the friendship and following of many. In 1541 this group of friends formed the Society of Jesus, or the Jesuits. At the age of 50, Ignatius was elected as the society's first general.[9] The society's ministerial focus was primarily education. Ignatius himself believed in "interior self-reform"[10] as the pathway to Christlikeness (as *The Spiritual Exercises* indicates). In order to share these and many other important truths, the society took on educating people of all ages. Members of the society were held to the strictest standards and

---

8. Romans 8:28.
9. Catholic Encyclopedia online, <http://www.newadvent.org/cathen/14081a.htm>. Accessed November 23, 2007.
10. Ibid.

were expected to watch their conduct closely. The *General Examen of Conscience* was an example of an exercise that would help a member take stock of their daily life, attitudes, and actions.

It is easy to understand how persons outside a strict order like the Society of Jesus could quickly lose the discipline (or never even consider the practice) that was required to do the difficult work of the daily, sometimes agonizing, inspection of one's own life and actions. For this reason it is not difficult to understand why the *General Examen* is not widely recognized or even practiced today.

Our Daily Lives

So often our lives are filled with continuous activity from the moment we awake till we collapse in exhaustion at the end of the day. So many of us have a multitude of demands and roles (co-worker, student, husband, father, son, and so on) we deal with everyday. Every waking moment is filled with responsibilities. Finding the time and having the energy to do the demanding labor required by the *Examen* can be quite intimidating. After all, when my life is constantly busy I do not have time to deal with the pain and disappointment that may be hiding just under the surface (which could arise in a moment or two of reflection). So instead of slowing down to consider how I am living, I keep the pedal down and speed through life, hoping someday to find a safe place to stop and rest. I "plug in" each day to get around having to speak to someone I want to avoid. I text instead of calling the person whom I acted impatiently with in fear they may confront me. I drive instead of walking the short distance I need to travel so as to desperately try and keep up with the hectic pace my life requires.

Intentionally slowing down to reflect on one's life is not a luxury afforded only to those cloistered in some hilltop monastery in Italy. No, rather it is an absolute essential *discipline* of anyone wanting to follow in the steps of Jesus Christ more authentically. When we move so quickly through life, we easily miss the ways in which we fall short in our mundane interactions with people. The careless word spoken because we were late, or the lack of patience with a child attempting to articulate something they found important, or a judgmental attitude toward a colleague who seems to have ample time to linger in conversation when deadlines approach. All these are examples that can be missed in the rush of life when we do not slow down to reflect, which is exactly what the *Examen* invites us to do.

Making personal reflection a regular input in one's own spiritual formation is vital to guard against developing a callous exterior toward others. The apostle Paul instructs us not to be mistaken about the importance that Christ places upon not only our actions, but even our motives, which are often secret to everyone but ourselves. 1 Corinthians 4:5b explains the final judgment, saying that God will *"bring to light what is hidden in darkness and will expose the motives of men's* (and women's) *hearts."* Our motivation must come under the Lordship of Christ every bit as much as our actions. All of our thoughts, actions, and motives must be submitted to Jesus' reign in our lives. We can become master rationalizers—particularly without accountability and personal reflection upon our daily encounters with others. However, with a regular time of Spirit-empowered personal reflection where God is invited into our reflecting and asked to point out our shortcomings, we can develop sensitivity to God's Spirit. This not only exposes our tendencies toward selfishness (sin), but also begins to enable us to avoid those pitfalls.

When we actively solicit His Spirit as we look over our day or week, we will be guaranteed to see some of our attitudes and actions that are not pretty. We must invite Christ into a personal encounter with ourselves. Who is a better accountability partner than Jesus Christ himself? It's one thing to ask a close friend for his or her perspective about our actions in a particular situation; it's very different to ask Christ His. Jesus not only sees things from our perspective, but also from the other person's! There is no other friend who is able to do that. Further, Jesus has our best interests in mind. Other friends may or may not. They may be dealing with their own needs, issues, and shortcomings (this is not an argument against personal accountability with a friend, which is vital. It's just a reality of our human condition).

So, how can we begin to incorporate the *General Examen* in our daily, weekly, or monthly routine of personal spiritual formation? Read on!

Rediscovering the Practice

Although many may find Ignatius' *General Examen of Conscience* to be useable right out of the box, not everyone will. For this reason, I would like to suggest a new way of viewing these five points and some additional factors that might better prepare a brother or sister in Christ to use this important practice.

A slight reworking of the *Examen* language becomes the following:

- *First*, begin this practice in a spirit of thanks. Take several moments to focus on God and all He has done for you today (air to breathe, food to eat—not to mention His salvation and love) and thank Him.

- *Second*, invite Jesus to help you to become more aware of your selfish and sinful behavior and to turn from it. Spend a few moments preparing your heart to look at this area more closely.

- *Third*, spend as long as it takes to recount your day, from first waking up until now. Think closely about each interaction, your thoughts, words, and actions. Look for unpleasant attitudes and ungodly actions for the purpose of overcoming these in your life.

- *Fourth*, invite Jesus into these broken places you have discovered to forgive, heal, and strengthen you for His purposes.

- *Fifth*, ask for God's strength to change and live as Christ. Close with the Lord's Prayer (Matt. 6:9-13).

To earnestly take up this practice will not be easy. Be assured that in exerting the necessary discipline it will take to do the *Examen*, you will be working in partnership with God's very powerful and gentle Spirit to renovate your soul.

Allow me to suggest some things that may prove to be useful. *First*, it will be essential to find a quiet place away from others and any source of interruption. I would strongly suggest turning off your cell phone, unplugging your iPod, and generally finding a place of solitude in which to begin this practice. *Secondly*, it could be helpful for you (as it is to me) to light a small candle as a symbol of God's presence while you embark on this very humbling journey of self inspection. *Third*, do not attempt to do the *Examen* without ample time to invest. I cannot imagine doing any justice to these five steps in any less than 30-45 minutes. *Finally*, you might find it useful to keep a journal or some sort of log to track the kind of things that you find are places of weakness. This journal/log may open your eyes to reoccurring sins and specific areas of struggle. This account that is created will serve as a caution for you in entering similar circumstances and alert you to places that you may not be well advised to enter. It could also help you see your spiritual progress as you watch how God enables you to conquer areas of struggle. In time, as you begin to know yourself and your tendencies toward sin better, this will enable you to have greater success in living a life pleasing to God.

If you find that after practicing the *Examen* consistently (exactly what is meant by "consistent" is up to the reader but I would suggest at least weekly for 6-8 weeks) there are particular sins in your life that are persistent and not seeming to diminish in frequency (or even increasing), do not be discouraged. This sort of growth can take time and long-term commitment to overcome. Spiritual maturation does not occur in a few weeks. It, like physical maturity, is a long-term process. Often it comes very slowly. At times it comes in spurts. Yet, given the right input, it *will* come.

Don't Walk Alone

The Christian life is not an individual sport; there is not a single technique that will guarantee success—especially quick success. Often it is the persistent discipline that moves us forward over the long term. Further, inviting others into our journey can prove vital. Finding like-minded individuals with whom you can share both your struggles and triumphs is necessary to ensure your own sanity and faithfulness. No one, including Jesus Christ, walks this path alone, so do not attempt to do so by yourself.

You may want to seek out another brother or sister (my strong suggestion is that it would be a person of your same gender) with whom to practice this discipline. The two of you could meet weekly, *after* your own private time of completing the *Examen*, to share your findings. Pray for each other and hold one another accountable on issues important to your lives. Obviously, it is not essential to share every detail of the *Examen* with one another. However, as this friendship grows and trust is proven, you may find that you are drawn to do that very thing.

The people with whom I have had close, accountable relationships know *everything* about my life. They know it all, and still they love me and accept me as I am. These are the brothers that have been Jesus Christ to me. They have proven invaluable to my growth in Christlikeness and my ability to accept and love myself.

Final Thoughts

The *Examen* was created by a once very sinful man. He became well acquainted with his own faults. I believe that it was through this understanding, coupled with God's grace, that he overcame his past and grew so much that many now remember him as *Saint* Ignatius.

JESUS PRAYER

By Josh Kleinfeld

The shout was desperate, loud, and clear. "Jesus, Son of David, have mercy on me!" It was repeated even louder, "Jesus, Son of David, have mercy on me!" However, the shouts were drowned out by the crowd that clamored around Jesus. Many in the crowd heard the man's cry and told him to "be quiet!" Who was this person shouting above the noise of the crowd? He was a blind beggar named Bartimaeus. Each day he was led outside the walls of Jericho to sit with the other beggars. He practiced this daily routine in order to earn what little cash he could from charitable people passing by. He had forgotten what it was like to see the sun rise in the morning. He relied on the help of others to make it through the streets and to earn a living. He was considered useless and cursed by society. At the time when Bartimaeus lived, people believed that the blind were condemned by God and were looked down upon with pity.

It is no wonder that when he heard it was Jesus walking by the place where he was sitting, he could not contain himself. Jesus was the guy who could heal people using His hands, His words, His breath, even His spit. He might have thought, "If Jesus healed others, why not me?"

Defying the crowd, Bartimaeus yelled at the top of his lungs, "Jesus, Son of David, have mercy on me!" Over and over again he yelled in desperation. Jesus heard him and asked, "What do you want me to do for you?" Bartimaeus did not have to think twice about this question. Eagerly he said, "Rabbi, I want to see." Jesus saw Bartimaeus' desperate faith and healed him, changing his life forever.

The Prayer of Jesus *(Lord Jesus Christ, have mercy on me)* is a standard prayer spoken repeatedly for the purpose of focusing on God and our need for His presence in our life. This prayer has three primary roots. One is found in the story you just read from Mark 10:46-52, another in understanding the power of the name of Jesus, and the third in a command given by the apostle Paul. These three roots intertwine to give us a practice that is both easily accessible and totally loaded with depth.

In the first root, found in the story above, we see that Bartimaeus had a sense of desperation which caused him to throw caution out the window. His life was broken and Jesus was his only hope. The realization of this led to a desperate cry which, ultimately, led to healing. This transformative encounter serves as a compelling reminder that when we cry out to Jesus, He hears our cry and responds. The second root comes from some instructions Paul wrote in a letter to the church in Thessalonica. On his second missionary journey, Paul was only able to teach there for a short time due to the violent persecution of the Jews. This left the church with little understanding of exactly how to follow the way of Jesus. In light of this, Paul provided guidance from a distance through letters. As he wrapped up his first letter, he gave the church a series of brief commands. Among these commands was the instruction to "pray without ceasing." Yes, you read that correctly; pray without stopping. Paul was saying there are no red lights in the prayer life of a Christian.

For Paul, to be in prayer was to be in current with Christ, the spring of infinite life. To pray was to live. To be connected to Christ "who is *your life*" (Col. 3:4) was as necessary as the blood in a person's vein. This command to continuously pray has left Christians reeling for centuries. Just how can we pray continuously? How do we fix our attention so much on God that we pray without ceasing, especially in a world that seems to be full of distractions?

The third root of the Prayer of Jesus comes from the understanding that the name of Jesus holds mysterious power. It was by His name that His followers exorcised demons, restored sight, and raised people from the dead. At one point Jesus told His disciples "You will ask me for anything in my name, and I will do it" (John 14:14). We see this in action in Acts 3 where Peter and John are greeted by a crippled beggar outside the Temple. He asked for money, which they didn't have, so they gave him what they did have. Peter said, "In the name of Jesus Christ of Nazareth, walk!" BAM! The man jumped up and his legs became strong enough for him to leap around the temple courts with joy. Can you imagine being a person who saw Peter heal the crippled beggar in the name of Jesus? You would be convinced that there was something mysteriously powerful about the name that Peter used.

So with these scriptures in the background, the Prayer of Jesus began to take shape. The earliest evidence of the practice of cease-less prayer came to us from fifth-century Egyptian monasteries. They prayed frequent one-word prayers that one theologian[11] called "arrow prayers," because they were like darts thrown to heaven. While they did practice ceaseless prayer, Jesus' name was not frequently used in the prayers. The first person to write about praying the name of Jesus unceasingly was St. Diadochus of Photice; he regularly whispered "Lord Jesus" over and over again. Shortly after Diadochus, other writers began using "Lord Jesus Christ, have mercy on me" and "Lord Jesus Christ, Son of God, have mercy on me" as a prayer.

According to the Eastern Orthodox tradition, there are general-ly three levels to the Jesus Prayer. The first is the verbal repetition of the phrase. The person who is praying speaks the request many times over. In order to keep focus, many use a *chotki*, or prayer rope (we will talk about how to do this later in the chapter). The second stage is when the prayer is repeated in the mind without distraction of other thoughts. The final stage is when the prayer connects the mind with the heart, so that the prayer lives in every heartbeat of the person praying.

Rediscovering the Prayer of Jesus

Many people have found this prayer to be an effective way to stay in constant contact with our loving Creator. Yet, there are sev-eral reasons why you do not hear the Prayer of Jesus used frequent-ly within the Protestant tradition.

Eastern Orthodoxy

One of the primary reasons that Protestants have lost touch with the Prayer of Jesus is due to the fact that this practice is large-ly supported by the Eastern Orthodox Church. As the Church grew through the first thousand years of its existence, two cities, Rome in the West and Constantinople in the East, struggled to gain ulti-mate control of the Church and its theology.[12] In 1054 a weird thing happened: the leaders of both churches decided to excom-municate (kick out) the other church's leaders. Yes, it was a dou-

---

11. A theologian is one who studies God and the things of God.
12. Theology is the study of God and the things of God.

ble excommunication. This meant that both the Roman church and the Constantinople church viewed themselves as the true church and the other as a false church. Two streams of Christianity came out of this split; Roman Catholicism and Eastern Orthodoxy. As the two drifted apart, each developed distinct theologies (beliefs) and spiritual practices. One of the dominant spiritual practices of the Eastern Orthodox Church became the Jesus Prayer. However, since Protestantism branched from the Roman Catholic Church, Protestants were left without the legacy of the Prayer of Jesus.

Could You Repeat That!?

Some use Jesus' condemnation of pagans who offered up "vain repetitions" (Matthew 6:7 KJV) as an objection to the Prayer of Jesus. However, some Bible scholars believe Jesus was not talking about repeated prayers directed to God. It was quite common for a Gentile (a person who is not Jewish) to pray to every god on their list. Essentially, they wanted to cover all their bases, so they prayed to every single god they knew of. Since there were a great number of idols available in Jesus' day, this would mean that a person could be praying for quite a length of time. Jesus' instruction didn't condemn repetitive prayer. It invited them to stop the stressful babbling the pagans felt was needed in order to appease every single god. Jesus clearly did not oppose repeated prayers, because He prayed a repeated prayer in the Garden of Gethsemane when He prayed "Not my will, but yours."

Keep in mind, repetition does not create some magical experience. If we view the Jesus Prayer as a way to get God on our side, a way to accomplish what we want, or a way of paying a debt to God then we need to reconsider our motivation. This prayer is meant to be a desperate appeal to a merciful God. If we see ourselves like the blind beggar Bartimaeus, begging for God's mercy, then we are in step with the traditional prayer.

That's for the Monks

Those who practice the Prayer of Jesus among the Eastern Orthodox have generally been monks or pilgrims. A typical monk takes a vow of celibacy (sexual abstinence) and commits to living with a monastic community. If you have ever been on the grounds of a monastery, it is hard not to notice the sense of peace that pervades the place. It is almost like time slows down. In this environment, monks are set up perfectly to spend hours and hours in prayer. It is not uncommon for a monk to take a vow of silence (going for long periods without speaking to anyone) in order to listen closely to God. Some monks have been known to observe silence for years on end!

Could you see this happening in your life? Imagine taking a vow of silence and going to school. Your teacher calls on you and you have to write on a note card, "I have taken a vow of silence. I won't be talking for the next two years." Most of us have distractions from the moment we wake up. A teen's life is full of activities and commitments. I know students that, while doing their homework, are watching their favorite show, texting friends, and updating their MySpace® page. With lives full of distractions, there is a growing need for students to find ways to connect with God apart from the craziness of life.

Praying the Jesus Prayer Today

This prayer is not for the faint of heart. This prayer is for those who know that they cannot face life without God. This prayer is for those who want to go deeper and want to experience the power of God in every single aspect of their life. This prayer is for those who want to take seriously Paul's call for unceasing prayer and to make prayer not just part of their life, but all of their life. If you are one of those people, I invite you to respond to the mercy of God and take on the challenge of the Jesus Prayer.

Traditional Ways to Pray the Jesus Prayer

The questions of the early Christians are the same for us today. *How do we pray continuously? How do we fix our attention that much on God? How do we do this in the midst of the crazy world in which we maneuver?*

Eliminating Distractions

One of the keys to living the Prayer of Jesus is finding time to pray, free from any distraction. The church fathers who wrote about this practice suggest praying in a dimly lit room, with minimum noise, and eyes closed. I use a candle to keep the room dimly lit. This candle symbolizes the presence of God in the room with me. I make sure to minimize any noise. It means removing anything extra that can be a distraction. (Yes, this means unplugging that MP3 player that has attached itself like a leech to your ear.) Music is awesome, but as you practice the Jesus Prayer it can take your attention away from God and turn it toward the music that is playing. Finding a place where you won't be bothered for a few minutes, and can sit quietly in the presence of God, will help you focus your attention exclusively on your connection with Him. This time of focus will actually help you stay concentrated on God throughout the rest of your day or week.

After you've found a quiet place, consider using one of the practices below.

Breathing Prayers

Basic biology: Our physical bodies require the regular intake of oxygen. Without it we would not survive. Basic spirituality: Our spirits require a bond with God. Without Him we are dead inside, rotten, and cold. Centuries ago, followers of Christ connected these two basic ideas and brought prayer life and breathing into harmony. We need God even more than we need the breath in our lungs. Praying a breath prayer is relatively simple once you get the hang of it.

For those who choose to say "Lord Jesus Christ, have mercy on me."

Breathe In: "Lord Jesus Christ. . ."
Breathe Out: "have mercy on me."

For those who choose to say "Lord Jesus, Son of David, have mercy on me."

Breathe In: "Lord Jesus, Son of David. . ."
Breathe Out: "have mercy on me."

You may be like me and find it difficult to speak as you are breathing in. I have found it easier to mouth the words, emphasizing them with my lips and tongue.

The beauty of breath prayers is you can do this anywhere you are breathing (which, if you did not know, is pretty much everywhere except underwater). One of my favorite locations for praying the Jesus Prayer in breath form is in front of the sink as I do the dishes. You can incorporate this form of prayer into your workout time, your study time, your chore time, your quiet time, your video game time, your dinner time, your youth group time, your date time, your nap time. . . are you getting the picture?

Chotki or Prayer Rope

I am the type of person who loves to have something in his hands. For instance, when I was in school I took Silly Putty with me to class. I played with that stuff so much during class it developed a stench. Even today, I constantly fiddle with my phone so much that it has a permanent circle worn into the center where I spin it. So, I have found the prayer rope to be excessively helpful in focusing my prayers.

A *chotki*, or prayer rope, looks like a necklace made of many knots with a cross on the end. (See Fig. 1) The traditional Eastern

Fig. 1

Orthodox *chotki* knots are intricately tied with nine cross-knots. However, there are other prayer ropes that have wooden or glass beads, rather than knots. Praying the Jesus Prayer with the prayer rope is fairly simple.

- Decide ahead of time how many times you want to pray the prayer. I recommend 10.
- Simply pray the Prayer of Jesus for each knot or bead that corresponds with the number of times you decide to pray the prayer.
- Don't rush. Linger on the words.

Some prayer ropes are broken up into sections with a larger bead or knot. (See Fig. 2)

Here is how I pray with my prayer rope:

- For each bead, I recite the Prayer of Jesus.

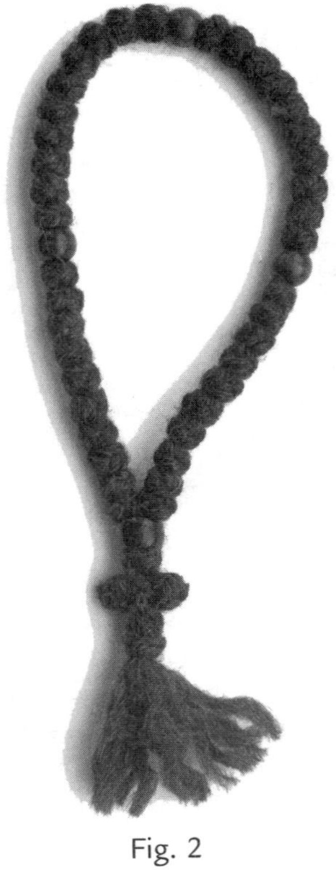

Fig. 2

🐦 At each of the larger beads I quote, "Abide in me, and I will abide in you" (John 15:4).

Feel free to change the scripture, but make sure it is something you can easily memorize. Here are other verses I would suggest:

"Be still and know that I am God" (Psalm 46:10).

"Be strong and courageous" (Josh. 1:9).

"It is for freedom that Christ has set us free" (Gal. 5:1).

I generally take my prayer rope with me during the day so that if I get any down time I can pray through it. Actually, I use it on my way to and from work. (If you would like to order a prayer rope you can find them online.)

Body Position

As we can see from the breath prayers, it can be said in any location and in any position. However, some have found it helpful to pray this prayer using different bodily positions. Here are a few examples you can choose from:

When reciting the prayer:

🐦 Kneel, bowing your face to the ground for every repetition. This behavior was typical for people greeting someone in authority over them. What a great way to tell God, and remind ourselves, that He has power over our lives.

🐦 Kneel with your arms outstretched. This is the position of a child waiting for his parent to pick him up. As you recite the prayer, allow God to remind you of His great Fatherly love for you.

🐦 Sit with your hands resting on knees, palms up. This is the position of a person peacefully waiting to receive whatever God has for them.

Dealing with Mental Distractions

Unless you are spiritually gifted, you are going to encounter significant mental and spiritual distractions when you first attempt this prayer (or any prayer, for that matter). You will find your mind wandering to sports scores, homework assignments looming over your head, or the argument you had with your parents. These thoughts aren't wrong, but they are distractions from your connection with God. If these thoughts arise, do not beat yourself up. Say to God, "take these thoughts," while at the same time bringing your focus back to the words you are saying. Sometimes I have found that the thoughts inside my head are so loud that I have to say my prayers at the top of my lungs.

As you verbally repeat the Prayer of Jesus, the words will begin to form in your mind as you continue on with the tasks of normal life. What begins to happen is that the prayer becomes embedded in your spirit. The prayer will rise up in you as you walk down the halls of your school, as you sit in the bus, and as you interact with people on the job.

Creative Ways to Pray the Jesus Prayer

Written

What if you could bring the Jesus Prayer to school by writing it in the margins of your notes? Maybe you don't have to write the entire thing, but you could just write the initials. People may wonder what *LJC (Lord Jesus Christ) HMOM (have mercy on me)* means, but it could serve as a reminder that at every moment you desperately need the mercy of Jesus Christ.

Praying Through Your Phone

The first cell phone I ever saw was the type that looked more like a purse than anything else. Today, it seems like everybody has a cell phone. I have often wondered if the phone could be used in spiritual ways. I think it can. Take a scroll through your contact list. As each person's name is highlighted, pray the Prayer of Jesus for that person. It is amazing what happens when you pray this prayer for others. God will begin to rework your perspective on people and help you to see them in the loving way He does.

Final Thoughts

A word of caution: the Prayer of Jesus is only one of many types of prayer that we can incorporate into our lives. We should still spend time daily in petition; presenting our needs and requests before God. There is still the need to daily praise and thank God for who He is and all He has done and is doing. We should still take time daily to listen to God; allowing His presence to infiltrate our lives. The purpose of this chapter was not designed to totally change the way you pray or communicate with God. Neither was the purpose to replace your firmly held beliefs about prayer. The goal is to introduce you to the Prayer of Jesus and expose you to another way you can talk with God and express your desire for His presence in your life.

However you choose to incorporate the Prayer of Jesus into your life, I pray that you call out to God like Bartimaeus. Pray that God would give you a thick sense of His presence and the love and strength to do the things He is calling you to do.

PRAYING SCRIPTURE

By Mickey E. Cox

"To pray the Scriptures is to order one's time of
prayer around a particular text in the Bible . . . a
particular Scripture influences the words, mood and
structure of my time with God."
—Evan B. Howard[13]

Familiar Roads

As I have read God's written Word for several years now, I am
discovering an incredible human connection of genuineness and
vulnerability in the pages of the Old and New Testaments, especially in the area of spiritual formation. One of those key areas is
prayer. There are numerous ways of praying, but all seem to have
a common base for us as followers—communicating with God.
That's good news for me as I step out into new ways of prayer and
communication with God. However, as I am on a spiritual journey,
like all of you, my tendency is to stay on familiar roads that I've
traveled many times, including in my spiritual life. Doing things
that are familiar and safe gives me a sense of security—maybe for
you as well.

Veering away from the familiar path enables me to move away
from the world and its grasp on my life. I'm always up for something that will take me away from the "produce and consume"
mentality and lifestyle of the world. However, this veering can lead
to some anxiety in the way I deal with the world, as well as my spiritual formation. Capitalism seems to rule my world. I've been
taught my life is supposed to focus around end results and bottom
lines. Activities in my life are supposed to produce results that I can
say I either accomplished, conquered, or that I'm capable of consuming. However, the reality of my journey with God is that I

---

13 Howard, Evan, B., *Praying the Scriptures* (Downers Grove: InterVarsity Press, 1999), 11.

should not look at spiritual formation as a "produce and consume" project, nor as something to be mastered like I do in other areas of my life, such as subjects in school or learning to play a sport or instrument. I must begin to understand that I'm not in control of what God wants to do in my life and must allow Him to take control of all aspects of my spiritual life as well.

With this in mind, praying Scripture needs to be looked at in the same way. That is, I must allow God to do in my life what He wants to do in order to draw me closer to Him. Praying Scripture is a very old practice. Basically, it means taking a passage from the Bible and making it one of my own prayers. Praying Scripture is a way of entering deeply into the passage with a heart alert to a unique and personal word from God.

As I read, reflect or meditate, pray, and contemplate the Scripture in silence with God, I allow God to transform me. I pray the Scripture, or use contemplative prayer, with the desire to simply draw closer to God. I am not practicing this spiritual discipline because I want to demand anything of God, such as what He will do for me or what He will give me. No, it's to know Him better and to express myself in ways that resonate with what my brothers and sisters in the past have written in Scripture.

New Road to Travel

If I continue to play the games I've played in the past, the way the world has conditioned me to, then I will try to control my life as well as the things around me. However, I must be willing to travel a new road—one less taken. I must be willing to read, meditate, pray, and contemplate the Scripture. I must be patient and listen in silence to God. Psalm 62:1 says, *"For God alone my soul waits in silence"* (NRSV).

To consistently travel the road of praying the Scriptures, I must start with what my friend Richard Foster has written about in his book, *Prayer*.

"Today the heart of God is an open wound of love. He aches over our distance and preoccupation. He mourns that we do not draw near to him. He grieves that we have forgotten him. He weeps over our obsession with muchness and manyness. He longs for our presence.

And he is inviting you—and me—to come home, to come home to where we belong, to come home to that for which we were created. His arms are stretched out wide to receive us. His heart is enlarged to take us in. The key to this home, this heart of God, is prayer."[14]

I must accept this invitation to journey on a new and different road and resist the temptation to take the path the world has constantly offered me to travel. You and I must do all we can to draw closer to this God who created us and brought us back into a right relationship with Him through the person of Jesus Christ. He desires that we communicate with Him, drawing closer to Him on a regular basis. If I travel this road, then I will discover this great God who loves me far more than I can ever understand in this earthly life.

Our Jewish Heritage

Jewish prayer traditions are a good place for us to start. In the Jewish tradition, we find that the *Siddur*, or Jewish Prayerbook, is used consistently for praying throughout the day. The prayers in the *Siddur* are based on Scripture, as well as Jewish teachings. The *Siddur* contains biblical prayers that go as far back as 3300 years, and prayers by rabbis that were based on Scripture composed 2500 years ago. These prayers are recited at different times throughout the day, starting with the morning blessings in a synagogue service and ending with evening prayers. This is the prayerbook that Jesus most likely used. Jesus was very familiar with the whole of the *Tanach*. *Tanach* is a Hebrew acronym for *Torah* (the first five books of the Old Testament), *Nevi'im* (the prophets), and *Kesuvim* (the wisdom, poetry, and historical books). Through reading and teaching the *Tanach*, Jesus was able to bring people closer to a true understanding of God.

In the past, I had heard of praying the Scriptures. However, it wasn't until I heard that Jewish prayers were filled with scriptural language—especially from the psalms and prophets—that it began to dawn on me that I could use these written prayers for my own spiritual life. These are often overlooked today because we think prayers always need to be spontaneous. It is intriguing to me to know that even the *Siddur* contains written introductory prayers composed of selected biblical verses. The following is customarily said prior to the

---

14. Foster, Richard. *Prayer: Finding the Heart's True Home* (San Francisco: HarperSanFrancisco, 1992), 1.

blessing and prayer for the end of the Sabbath, and is an example of the type of prayer we can use while praying Scripture.

"'Surely God is my salvation; I will trust and not be afraid. The LORD, the LORD, is my strength and my song; he has become my salvation.' With joy you will draw water from the wells of salvation" (Isaiah 12:2-3). "From the LORD comes deliverance. May your blessing be on your people. Selah" (Psalm 3:8). "The LORD Almighty is with us, the God of Jacob is our fortress. Selah" (Psalm 46:11).

Most Jewish prayers come from the book of Psalms, as well as from other great prayers written in Scripture. For example, Moses prayed that God would forgive Israel (Exodus 32:31-32) and Jonah prayed from the belly of the fish (Jonah 2:2-9). These, along with many other Old Testament prayers, are worth reading, reflecting on, praying, contemplating, and memorizing in order to absorb the words as I continue the journey of spiritual formation. Also, having conversations with God about the promises in Scripture is another important Jewish prayer tradition.

Jesus and Scripture

Since individuals did not own copies of Scripture until more recent times, they would gather in the Temple or synagogues to hear Scripture read. It was in this setting that Jesus made His most profound declaration of himself. Following His reading from the scroll of Isaiah (61:1-2), Jesus said, *"The Spirit of the Sovereign Lord is on me, because the Lord has anointed me to preach good news to the poor. He has sent me to bind up the brokenhearted, to proclaim freedom for the captives and release from darkness for the prisoners, to proclaim the year of the Lord's favor"* (Luke 4:14-21). He concluded His reading of Isaiah by saying to those gathered in the synagogue, *"Today this scripture is fulfilled in your hearing."* Jesus was connecting this reading of prophetic Scripture, regarding the Messiah, to His current situation. For us today, there can be an amazing connection between God's Word and our lives if we are willing to put praying Scripture into practice.

The Early Church

In the Early Church, believers were taught to continue to pray scriptures, just as they had done with the *Siddur*. They believed that praying Scripture connected them to the mind and heart of God.

In the Jewish tradition, when Scripture was repeatedly prayed, it became memorized. This was of benefit for those who could not read or did not have access to Scripture like we do today.

The Early Church used praises, petitions, and intercessions found in the *Tanach*. These are scattered throughout the Bible and can be used in our praying Scripture and contemplation time. For example, we read in John 12:32, *"You said that you would draw all men to yourself!"* We then can turn around and pray, *"Father, draw Jim closer to yourself that he may know you more fully."* The use of our creative imagination to envision spiritual thoughts adds to praying Scripture. For instance, *"He sits enthroned above the circle of the earth, and its people are like grasshoppers. He stretches out the heavens like a canopy, and spreads them out like a tent to live in"* (Isaiah 40:22). I don't know about you, but my mind's eye can "see" what Isaiah is writing. I can take this passage of Scripture and place God in this same setting in our world today.

Where Do I Begin?

1. Begin by praying for God to open up His Word to you. Ask the Holy Spirit to open up your heart and mind. Consider sitting quietly, anticipating the presence of God to lead you.

2. Next, read the passage of Scripture. Reading it serves as a mirror for us. Just as my physical eye cannot see the food from lunch that is on my face without a mirror, so my spiritual eyes cannot discover God's truth without the reflection of Scripture. This is another way praying Scripture can help you in your journey with God.

3. Take time to think about what the passage is saying. Then read the passage again as a prayer. Make it personal by using "I" and "me." You may even want to insert others' names in the prayer if appropriate. Pray as if you had written the prayer yourself.

4. Consider reading the passage as a prayer several times. Take time between each prayer to contemplate, sitting quietly in God's presence and listening.

5. After time spent in prayer, feel free to write down any thoughts and feelings you have in a journal (see chapter 6). This way you can go back and see how God answered that prayer.

The Spiritual Benefits of Praying the Scripture

Praying Scripture can help us return to a simple way of openness and attentiveness to God. As we said at the beginning of this chapter, we must lay aside our own agendas and attitudes and open ourselves up to prayers in Scripture that God has given us. This time spent in prayer will allow us to focus on God and give us the opportunity to deeply connect with Him. For example, we can look at the prayers of Jesus (Matthew 6:9-13; Matthew 26:36-46; John 17), Paul (Ephesians 3:14-25; Colossians 1:9-12), Daniel (Daniel 2:19-23; Daniel 9:3-19), Mary (Luke 1:46-55), Moses (Exodus 33:12-17; Numbers 11:1-2, 10-15), and so on. These are prayers that can easily translate into our own prayers.

The Jewish nation, the early Christians, and the desert fathers all understood the value of the Bible as a source of prayers. Probably the best book to start with in praying Scripture is the Book of Psalms. This book confirms so clearly our humanness. It does not gloss over the difficulties of life, nor does it clean up the mess people have made of it. It brings out very clearly the fact that this is a journey. I've found it to unusually voice my needs, my fears, my joys and praises, my sorrows and anger, as well as my loneliness and spiritual dryness at times. As I read the Psalms, I am invited to be authentic and honest about my journey with God—coming to Him just as I am.

When I'm at a loss for words about my current situations, these passages of Scripture can guide me towards being real as I approach God. The words written in Psalms can provide me the help and structure that keep me on the path—through the ups and downs of my journey with Him. I truly believe that these prayers will awaken in you a deep Scripture-based connection with God like nothing you have known before. The beauty in these prayers is found in taking the words of brothers and sisters who have come before you, and making their prayers your own.

I have listed two Psalms for you to read and reflect upon, followed by some space below the passage to write out your own prayer from Scripture. Be sure to take your time. Although writing out our prayers in this manner is a little different from what those in the past have done, we are setting a pattern for our future in praying Scripture when our own words just will not come.

My Praying Scriptural Space

Psalm 5:1-3

"Give ear to my words, O LORD, consider my sighing. Listen to my cry for help, my King and my God, for to you I pray. In the morning, O LORD, you hear my voice; in the morning I lay my requests before you and wait in expectation."

My Prayer to God

Psalm 139:1-6

"O LORD, you have searched me and you know me. You know when I sit and when I rise; you perceive my thoughts from afar. You discern my going out and my lying down; you are familiar with all my ways. Before a word is on my tongue you know it completely, O LORD. You hem me in—behind and before; you have laid your hand upon me. Such knowledge is too wonderful for me, too lofty for me to attain."

My Prayer to God

Final Thoughts

Now that you've tried praying Scripture, continue to look at other passages for identification of your own journey with God. As you do, try reading the passages out loud, just like they did in the Jewish Temple and synagogues. Even when a person was alone, reading was done audibly for more of an impact on one's heart, mind, and soul. Hearing the sound of your own voice speaking the words of Scripture can have a stunning effect. Try this using the following passages:

Psalm 51
Psalm 84
Psalm 123

Psalm 141
Psalm 145
I Samuel 3:9
Lamentations 3:49-51
Acts 4:29-30
Jeremiah 17:14

Travel a new road on your journey with God. Don't look for that "produce and consume" end result of praying Scripture in your spiritual formation. Look for new ways in which God is speaking to you as you search through the Bible for prayers that will not only give you a deeper frame of reference, but a deeper and richer relationship with the One to whom those prayers were originally written.

For Further Reading on Praying Scripture

Beginning Contemplative Prayer by Kathryn J. Hermes. (Servant Publications)

Celebration of Discipline by Richard J. Foster. (HarperSan Francisco)

Entering God's Presence by Stephen D. Eyre. (InterVarsity Press)

Learning to Pray Through the Psalms by James W. Sire. (InterVarsity Press)

Scribbling in the Sand by Michael Card. (InterVarsity Press)

Spiritual Classics Edited by Richard Foster and Emilie Griffin. (HarperSan Francisco)

Spiritual Disciplines for the Christian Life by Donald S. Whitney. (NavPress)

Spiritual Disciplines Handbook by Adele Ahlberg Calhoun. (InterVarsity Press)

To Be a Jew by Rabbi Hayim Halevy Donin. (Basic Books, Inc., Publishers)

To Pray and to Love by Roberta C. Bondi. (Fortress Press)

Traditions of the Ancients by Marcia Ford. (Broadman and Holman Publishers)

LECTIO DIVINA

By Mike Wonch

During my junior high and senior high school years, I was required to read certain books for English class. (Ever heard of *Beowulf* or *Macbeth*?) These books were considered classics and must reads . . . according to my teachers. My teachers would spend time telling the class how important these books were and why we should read them. To be honest, I did read them, but got little (if anything) from their content. It wasn't until my senior year of college that I truly learned how to read literature in a meaningful way. My American Literature professor taught me how to read and understand literature in such a way that the words on the page spoke to me and had meaning for my life. Up to that point, I just read these books because my teacher said it was important and that I would supposedly learn something. When I began to approach literature the right way, classics written by Thoreau and Hawthorne began to have meaning, and I was able to understand how something written hundreds of years ago still spoke to me.

Over the years, I have observed people who have read the Bible, but received very little from it because they had a hard time understanding its message. I have also seen people avoid reading the Bible altogether because they could not understand how something written thousands of years ago had anything to say to them in the 21st century. Yet, the Bible was written to be read, to be understood, and, most importantly, to be transformational. So, how can we read Scripture in a way that it speaks to us with power? One way to read God's Word for meaning is through *lectio divina*. *Lectio divina* (pronounced lek-tsee-oh dih-vee-nuh), is a Latin phrase that means *sacred* or *divine reading*. The purpose of *lectio divina* is to pray and read Scripture in order to connect with God and allow the Holy Spirit to lead and guide you through its words. Through *lectio divina*, you approach God's Word anticipating that

He will speak through its message. In essence, *lectio divina "opens us to that deep level of communication with the Divine."*[15]

History of Lectio Divina

There is nothing new about hearing God's Word and allowing it to speak to our hearts. The early Israelites understood the importance of hearing and understanding God's Word. During the days of Moses, he reminded the people, *"the word is very near you; it is in your mouth and in your heart so you may obey it"* (Deut. 30:14). Part of their worship practice was to read the Scripture and pray in community (Nehemiah 8). This practice of reading, listening, and praying was passed on to future generations among the Jewish people. Although not specifically mentioned, we know that early Christians continued this tradition of reading Scripture and listening to God through His Word.

> *"But as for you, continue in what you have learned and have become convinced of, because you know those from whom you learned it, and how from infancy you have known the holy Scriptures, which are able to make you wise for salvation through faith in Christ Jesus"* (2 Timothy 3:14-15).

Early Church leaders continued the practice began by prior Christian brothers and sisters. The Bible scholar, Origen (around the year A.D. 220), emphasized reading the Bible by way of attention, constancy, and prayer. He believed in the importance of Scripture reading and urged *"his students to set aside a significant part of each day for study, meditation and prayer."*[16] During the Monastic period, Christians further developed this into the practice of reading, meditating, contemplating, and praying the Scripture. In the 12th century, a monk named Gugio II wrote *The Ladder of the Monks*. In this, he describes four steps to approaching Scripture: reading, meditation, prayer, and contemplation. He says, *"Reading seeks for the sweetness of a blessed life, meditation perceives it, prayer asks for it, contemplation tastes it."*[17]

John Wesley (18th century theologian and founder of Methodism) similarly continued this practice during his day. In the preface of the *Explanatory Notes upon the Old Testament*, written in 1765, he wrote about this effective way to read Scripture.

---

15. Hall, Thelma. *Too Deep For Words: Rediscovering Lectio Divina* (New York: Paulist Press), 7.

16. Hall, Christopher A. *Reading the Scriptures with the Church Fathers* (Downers Grove: InterVarsity Press, 1998), 142.

17. Guigio, translated by Edmund Colledge and James Walsh. *The Ladder of Monks and Twelve Meditations* (Kalamazoo: Cistercian Publications, 1979), 68.

1. Set apart a little time each morning and/or evening to read the Bible.
2. If time allows, read a chapter out of the Old Testament and one out of the New Testament. If time does not allow, read a single chapter, or a part of one.
3. Read the passage(s) with attentiveness in order to know God's will and the determination to do it.
4. Understand the connection between God's Word and your life as a disciple of Jesus Christ.
5. You should be in a continuous attitude of prayer.
6. As you read, you should take time to examine yourself by what you read, both with respect to your heart and life.
7. *"Whatever light you then receive, should be used to the uttermost, and that immediately. Let there be no delay. Whatever you resolve, begin to execute the first moment you can. So shall you find this word to be indeed the power of God unto present and eternal salvation."*[18]

When it came to the Bible, Wesley believed in *reading* (points 1, 2, and 3), *meditation* (point 4), *prayer* (point 5), and *contemplation* (points 6 and 7) in order to let the Word speak to and transform a person's heart and life.

Today, just as those who have traveled the God-path before us, there is still the need to allow God to speak to us through His Word. *"We must learn to attend to God's Word in Scripture. When our reading is thus listening to God, Holy Scripture becomes God's word of promise, or rebuke, or counsel, or comfort, or whatever He sees we need. To pray as we read, and read as we pray—this is the proper approach to Holy Scripture."*[19] An ancient practice, *lectio divina* is a valuable way to read Scripture today.

The Practice of Lectio Divina

There are four elements to *lectio divina*: lectio, meditatio, oratio, and contemplatio. That is, reading, meditation, prayer, and contemplation. We will examine the importance of each.

Lectio (reading)

We do not just read the Scripture for information to be memo-

---

18. <http://wesley.nnu.edu/john_wesley/notes/otpreface.htm>. Accessed December 20, 2007.
19. Dunning, H. Ray and William Greathouse, *An Introduction to Wesleyan Theology* (Kansas City: Beacon Hill Press of Kansas City, 1989), 14.

rized; we read it to internalize and allow God to change us through its message. The way we read is a *"listening and a hearing, attuned to the inspired word and attentive to the Speaker."*[20] There is no skimming or casually glancing over the words. It is reading slowly, giving our full attention to the message in anticipation of hearing its timeless truth speak to our hearts. Michael Casey suggests that reading the Bible *"is like reading poetry: we need to slow down, to savor what we read, and to allow the text to trigger memories and associations that reside below the threshold of awareness."*[21] We must read the Bible with more than just our eyes. In a sense, we must read the Word with our ears as well.

When we read a magazine, we may or may not read it with our full attention. If we are in a hurry we may glance at what it says in an attempt to get the basic message of the article—not so with *lectio divina*. Here we read slowly, consciously, carefully, listening to hear what God said and is saying. Most times, God does not shout His message to us, but whispers it gently into our ears. If we are to read God's Word in order to hear His message, we must read it in such a way that we are able to listen rather than just glance over the words written on the page.

Meditatio (meditation)

Meditation is something that has been practiced since Old Testament times. David says in Psalm 119:10-16, *"I seek you with all my heart; do not let me stray from your commands. I have hidden your word in my heart that I might not sin against you. Praise be to you, O LORD; teach me your decrees. With my lips I recount all the laws that come from your mouth. I rejoice in following your statutes as one rejoices in great riches. I* ***meditate*** *on your precepts and consider your ways. I delight in your decrees; I will not neglect your word"* (emphasis added).

Meditation means the *"pondering of something: the act of thinking about something carefully, calmly, seriously, and for some time, or an instance of such thinking."*[22] It does not mean we empty our heads and

---

20. Hall, Thelma. *Too Deep For Words: Rediscovering Lectio Divina* (New York: Paulist Press, 1988), 36.

21. Casey, Michael. *Sacred Reading: The Ancient Art of Lectio Divina* (Missouri: Liguori Publications, 1995), 83.

22. <http://encarta.msn.com/dictionary_1861629027/meditation.html>. Accessed December 13, 2007.

allow anything and everything to fill our minds. When we read the Scripture, we take time to reflect on its message and meaning. For instance, say we read Jesus' words in John 10:14: *"I am the good shepherd; I know my sheep and my sheep know me."* We should not only take time to read the words, but also take time to think about what it means that Jesus is the Good Shepherd, what it means to be His sheep, and what He was saying about himself and about us.

Through meditation, we seek to find the face of God and what He wants to reveal to us through His Word. When we meditate, we do not go into some hypnotic state where we lose control of our senses. When we reflect on the Word, we allow its message to act together with our thoughts, feelings, and emotions in order to dwell on what God's Word is saying and meaning.

In our fast-paced world, we take little time for serious thinking. We watch television, listen to music, and read a magazine without really taking time to understand the messages we are putting into our minds. Meditation is slowing down to think about all the Word is saying to us.

Oratio (prayer)

Prayer involves both speaking and listening. It is an interaction with the Divine. Prayer is more than bringing our requests to God; it is inviting God to speak to us.

In *lectio divina*, prayer focuses on what we have read, and what our minds have focused on during meditation. It is a time of quiet listening, and a time of speaking when prompted by the Holy Spirit. Again, it is not an emptying of the mind, but a filling with the presence of God. This means when we encounter God, *"the longing of our heart spontaneously calls out to Him, or, realizing its infidelity and unworthiness, begs healing and mercy."*[23]

Prayer is a two-way communication between ourselves and God. It is a time when we speak to God and allow God to speak to us.

Contemplatio (contemplation)

This is the part of *lectio divina* where we rest in the presence of God. We listen to the voice of God in the silence of the moment.

---

23. Hall, *Too Deep For Words: Rediscovering Lectio Divina*, 42.

This means we begin to think about God, His Word, and how it can and does transform our lives. This, in turn, impacts the way we think and live. In other words, we take what we have read and understood and apply it to our daily lives. Mike King says that contemplation means, *"dwelling in God's presence, we contemplate how Scripture should impact our attitudes, actions and behavior."*[24]

Contemplation means opening ourselves up to God's leading. You should not leave the place where you are the same way you were before you entered into the presence of God. Through this encounter with God, *"there is a yielding of oneself to God's will. We resolve and act on the message of Scripture."*[25] Contemplation means allowing this experience, through the Holy Spirit, to change your life.

How to Experience Lectio Divina

We have seen what *lectio divina* is all about, but how do you actually put it into practice? *Lectio divina* can be experienced individually or in a group setting. (See chart on next page.)

An Example of Lectio Divina in Action

Here is an example of how *lectio divina* can be put into practice using Psalm 23.

Read: Read the passage once. Then read it again slowly.

Meditate: Read the passage one more time. As you read, look for words or phrases that stand out to you. (For example: "the Lord is my Shepherd", "guides", "leads", "comforts", and "dwell in the house of the Lord".) Think about what those words or phrases mean in your relationship with God. How is God the shepherd? How does He comfort, lead, and guide your life? How can you dwell in God's house?

Pray: Spend time in quietness. Listen to God's voice. Ask, "Lord, what are You saying to me through your Word?" Then, take time to pray. Praise God for being the Shepherd of your life. Confess those things you feel you need to confess. Thank God for leading and guiding your life. Close by praying for friends, family, and so on.

Contemplate: Think about how God guides your life. Write down

24. King, Mike. *Presence-Centered Youth Ministry*, (Downers Grove: InterVarsity Press, 2006), 149.

25. Cassell, Bo, ed. *Lectio Divina Bible Studies for Youth: Listening for God through Mark* (Kansas City: Barefoot Ministries, 2007), 6.

Lectio Divina Practice	Individual	Group Setting
Lectio (reading)	Choose a text of Scripture. (You may want to ask an older Christian to suggest a Bible passage to begin with.) The Scripture you choose should contain more than one verse. Read your text slowly. Be sure to listen for the voice of God as you read. Read these verses several times.	A passage of Scripture is chosen. The group leader reads the passage several times, allowing for people to think and reflect on the Word.
Meditatio (meditation)	Take a word or phrase that stands out and begin to think about its meaning. Ask, "What is God saying to *me* through these words?"	Read the passage again. Ask the group to listen for a word or phrase that speaks to them, and have them share with the rest of the group.
Oratio (prayer)	Pray. Simply listen to God. Ask God to penetrate your heart and mind. At first, you may have trouble knowing what or how to pray. One suggestion is to find a written prayer that speaks to you and expresses your thoughts and feelings. Read this written prayer as your prayer to God.	The passage is read for a final time. Pray, asking each person to pray silently for themselves, and then for the person on his or her left.
Comtemplatio (contemplation)	Rest. Take what you have learned and think about how to apply it to your life.	Conclude by asking group members to think about what the passage is saying to each of them and how they can apply the Word to their life.

several areas of your life where you need more of God's leading and guidance. Think of several things you can do that week to allow more of His presence in your life.

Keys to Understanding Lectio Divina

This way of reading Scripture may likely be a new concept to you. So here are a few thoughts to help before you begin the practice of *lectio divina*.

What Lectio Divina IS!

🐟 *A way to read God's Word for meaning, and not just for content*. This is not the only way to read God's Word. However, it is one way we can read the Word so that it opens the door for God to transform our lives. Michael Casey says it is a way of *"welcoming the word and to cherish and celebrate the manifold revelation of God, incarnate in the Scriptures."*[26]

🐟 *A specific time set aside to speak and listen to God*. Lectio divina gives you the opportunity to take time, get silent, and listen to God and His Word through the power of the Holy Spirit. It also allows you time to pray, and to really spend time speaking to God. Considering all the noise in our lives, getting quiet before God allows us to really communicate with and hear Him.

🐟 *A way to understand how to apply the Word to your life*. The Bible is more than words on a page. It is God's Word to us, meant to be lived out by those who call themselves His followers.

What Lectio Divina is NOT!

🐟 *Quick devotions*. Lectio divina takes time. It is not something that can be done in five minutes in the morning or just before you go to bed at night. It is something that takes commitment. You must decide to make time for *lectio divina*. In other words, it must become a priority.

🐟 *A magical formula*. Most likely, you will not experience a bright light beaming down on you, God speaking in an audible voice, and all your questions being answered. That is not to say this couldn't happen. However, understand that God speaks in many ways and in His time. *Lectio divina* is not a

---

26. Casey, *Sacred Reading: The Ancient Art of Lectio Divina*, 29.

formula where you add certain ingredients together to produce a specific result. It is a time of opening up the Word and allowing God to speak to you. Be patient, understanding that God does have something to say to you.

🌹 *A substitute for biblical & spiritual instruction. Lectio divina* is not a replacement for Bible study, Sunday School, or preaching. We still need biblical teaching from a pastor, leader, teacher, and Bible study resources. We must still take time to do Bible study, using a variety of study methods. This is done by *"reading and studying the Bible exegetically—thinking, evaluating, synthesizing data, reasoning, and giving attention to language, symbols, and context."*[27] In other words, *lectio divina* should not be the only type of Bible study you do.

Barriers to Lectio Divina

Although you may understand the need for getting into God's Word, there are many barriers that get in the way of actually reading the Bible. Being aware of them is the first step in not falling into their trap.

Busyness. Most adults I know run from one activity to another. Their lives are so filled that many are experiencing serious emotional stress. Pressure on their time squeezes them from all sides. Students' lives are no different. Walt Mueller says, *"Their [students'] lives are sometimes structured to the point where there is little 'free time.'"*[28] Our lives are so filled with things we are required to do, we have little time to do things we *like* or know we *should* do.

Most people do not spend time in God's Word because they feel they are too busy to read it, and do not have time to squeeze it into their already jam-packed schedule. *Lectio divina* must be an intentional commitment of time. This may mean other things have to take lesser priority in your life.

Cultural lens vs. biblical lens. Television, music, movies, and the internet all shout messages that reach your ears and mind. These messages have an impact on your life. Richard Dunn says, *"Our culture is flooded with deceptive messages about who God is, who we are and what is to be valued as truly meaningful."*[29]

27. King, *Presence-Centered Youth Ministry*, 140.
28. Mueller, Walt. *Engaging the Soul of Youth Culture* (Downers Grove: InterVarsity Press, 2006), 102.
29. Dunn, Richard. *Shaping the Spiritual Lives of Students* (Downers Grove: InterVarsity Press, 2001), 20.

It can be difficult to filter through all the messages you receive in a day's time. What is harmful and what is not can sometimes be hard to determine among all the messages you receive. You may not even realize the amount of information you are exposed to in any given day. We must make a conscious effort to filter cultural messages through a biblical lens. (That is, your beliefs and approach to every aspect of life are consistent with and/or originate from Scripture.) Developing a biblical lens begins by reading and understanding the message of God's Word.

Lack of understanding. You may know you need to read God's Word, but you may not know how to effectively do so. Many do not spend time reading the Bible simply because they do not feel they know how to read it. Reading and understanding the Bible is not always easy; however, *lectio divina* can be a step toward reading the Bible in a more meaningful way.

Final Thoughts

God's Word is meant for you today, as it was for those who lived during the time it was being written. God still has something to say to you, as He did to Moses and Paul. *Lectio divina* is a way for you to read the Bible with such an approach as to understand what God has to say and, through the Holy Spirit, allow His Word to speak to you and transform your life.

SOLITUDE/ MEDITATION

By Mike Kipp

If you grew up with siblings in your house then, undoubtedly, you know what it is like to want to be alone. This is particularly true for those of us that shared a room. There is something magnetic that draws us to long for time and space to be simply by ourself (however, if you were an only child, your desires may have been quite the opposite). For those of us who had multiple siblings and a single bathroom to accommodate everyone's needs, the desire to be alone could be especially strong! It could seem like there was never a moment to simply think your own thoughts, let alone be by yourself. From morning until night, your home and head could easily be filled with the noise of life. It is no wonder why many of us in these sorts of circumstances find our own "special places" of solitude somewhere. Whether it is in a hidden corner of the house, in a more remote part of our backyard, or in some other venue nearby, we all need our own time alone. We all seem to have an inherent desire for the time and space that allows for private reflection or for our purposes here, meditation. (Instead of explicitly stating "solitude/mediation" throughout this chapter, I will only mention solitude, but both will be implied. It is my conviction that these two are inextricably connected. It is in our times of solitude, although not exclusively, that we are enabled to do deep reflection upon all aspects of our lives. Similarly, when we are engaged in true meditation, we are often "isolated" from others— even when sitting adjacent to someone.)

Historical Background

In Jesus' life, we see this desire acted upon. The following snippets of verses from Matthew, Mark, and Luke illustrate the consistency with which Jesus got away from people to be alone. In Matthew 4 we read about the forty days Jesus spent in the desert alone (just prior to the beginning of His public ministry) in which He fasted and was tempted by the devil. Mark 1:35 tells us, *"Very early in the morning, while it was still dark, Jesus got up, left the house and went off to a solitary place, where he prayed."* Luke 5:16 describes clearly the regularity with which Jesus sought out solitude, *"But Jesus often withdrew to lonely places and prayed."* Finally, Luke 6:12 gives an example of the length of time Jesus spent in solitude. *"One of those days Jesus went out to a mountainside to pray, and **spent** the night praying to God"* (emphasis added). So we see demonstrated in the life of Christ the importance of solitude.

Early Christians took this example quite literally. In the late second and early third centuries, due to their perception that Christianity was becoming too watered down, Christians began to organize themselves into monastic orders. The earliest of these simply fled the cities to live alone (or in loosely associated groups) in the desert. Others formed monasteries where they lived a life in community, but isolated from the rest of society. Although the history of this movement is quite intriguing, it is beyond the scope of this chapter. Let me include one short story, however, that illustrates the lengths—obviously extreme at times—that individuals went to in order to seek solitude and prove their love for God. The following is an excerpt from Dallas Willard's book, *The Spirit of the Disciplines,* (a great book on the purposes of practicing the Spiritual Disciplines).

> *No one who has looked squarely upon the life of Jesus and the apostles can imagine them engaging in the strange behavior of a Macarius of Alexandria, or a Serapion, or a Pachomius: eating no cooked food for seven years, exposing the naked body to poisonous flies while sleeping in a marsh for six months, not lying down to sleep for forty or fifty years, not speaking a word for many years . . . explicitly vying with one another for the championship in austerities.*
>
> *Simeon Stylites (A.D. 389-459), for instance . . . found (a column) sixty feet high, three feet across, with a railing to prevent him from falling off in his sleep. On this perch Simeon lived uninterruptedly for thirty years, exposed to rain and sun and cold. A ladder enabled disciples to take him food and remove his waste. He bound himself to the pillar by a rope; the rope became embedded in his flesh, which putrefied around it, and stank, and teemed with worms. Simeon picked up the worms that fell from his sores, and replaced them there, saying to them, "Eat what God has given you."*[30]

---

30. Willard, Dallas. *The Spirit of the Disciplines: Understanding How God Changes Lives* (San Francisco: Harper, 1988), 142.

Obviously, these examples (beyond being nauseating) serve to illustrate those who have taken a good thing and become obsessed with it to the point of rendering the entire practice worthless, because it is no longer a means to an end but rather an end in itself. Even good things can become idols in our lives. In fact, we may be in more danger of making the good things we do "idols" in our lives over the not-so-positive things. After all, if a little is good, isn't a lot better?

While I deeply admire their passion and resolve, I see their behavior as seriously misdirected. It is likely due to examples like this that many Christians dismiss the entire idea of solitude—sort of throwing the baby out with the bathwater. When the historic expressions of solitude go to such extremes as living in isolation on a column sixty feet high or in some hilltop monastery in Brazil, it is easy to think that there is no possible way for me to do anything remotely similar to that. After all, I am a student, I live in a family, I have homework, a job, other responsibilities, and . . . I really like people!

Lost in Translation

With the rise of monasteries and convents throughout the next several centuries, coupled with their growing presence around the edges (and in the middle) of society, it was easy for people to make the assumption that solitude was something that monks and nuns practiced, but it was not something for those of us who were a part of mainstream society. However, when life was centered on the farm, there were still times when individuals would naturally experience regular periods of alone time. Whether it was performing chores in the barn or field, cooking, cleaning, walking or riding horseback from one place to another, or some other manual labor—life was not as noisy as it would become in the modern era.

With the rise of the industrial economy and a shift from agrarian (farm-centered) to an industrial (factory-centered) society, life became much louder and persons more akin to human "doings" than human "beings." Workers in these situations often labored long hours—12 to 16 or more—and even small children were employed in the dangerous work of the factories. Life had lost its natural rhythm provided by the seasons on the farm. No longer was there a time of planting, a time of growing, a time of harvest, and a time of rest. Now life and work were constant, loud, dirty, unsafe, and relentless. Solitude was likely not considered much, because finding the next meal or earning enough money for rent had taken first priority.

With the loss of this rhythm to life that was in-step with the seasons, life became much more about survival and doing than simply being (that was at least a part of the rhythm of life on the farm). Even when the industrial age became embedded into our culture and laws were passed that protected workers, and affluence was gained—we had forgotten how to be by ourselves. Life in the city was always moving, always noisy, always awake, and always beckoning us to join in frenetic hyperactivity that often characterizes life in the city. Even those who live outside of the city today find this hyperactive pace creeping into the once quieter environs of the suburbs. T.S. Eliot describes this pace as:

> Endless invention, endless experiment,
> Brings knowledge of motion, but not of stillness;
> Knowledge of speech, but not of silence;
> Knowledge of words, and ignorance of the Word . . .
>
> Where is the Life we have lost in living?
> Where is the wisdom we have lost in knowledge?
> Where is the knowledge we have lost in information?[31]

Today many other characteristics of our current culture interfere with finding time and space to ourselves. Whether it is the cell phone we cannot put down, the iPod we never turn off, the ubiquitous wireless connection on which we surf and "stay connected", or simply our own lack of comfort and familiarity with ourselves to be alone, we are continuously engaged in distraction. Because of these, and many other issues, we simply do not know what it is like to be intentionally alone (an irony of this way of life is that we often isolate ourselves from others near us as we communicate with someone who is apart from us), nor do we understand the great value that solitude and meditation can bring to our inner life,

---

31. Taken from T.S. Eliot's *Choruses from* "The Rock," *Collected Poems 1909-1935*, as quoted in Don Postema, *Space for God*, 15.

and thus our outer life too. When we do not take time to disengage, to unplug from the technology we live in, to find space for thoughtful reflection, do we really live? Do we routinely reflect on the events of our lives to discern both their value and meaning to our existence or is our life characterized primarily by events, one after another? Do we take time to notice what is taking place in our life and the lives of those around us?

In a scene from Thornton Wilder's play *Our Town*, Emily, a young woman who dies in childbirth, asks an important question in this vein. The stage manager gives her a unique opportunity to return from death in order to live one day of her life with her family over. She is disappointed with what she finds.

Emily: *We don't have time to look at one another. (She breaks down, sobbing.) I didn't realize. So all that was going on and we never noticed . . . do any human beings ever realize life while they live it—every, every minute?*

Stage Manager: *No, (Pause) The saints and poets, maybe—they do some.*[32]

What about you? Do you ever "realize life while you live it" or are you too busy to notice your own inner state, let alone that of those all around?

The value of choosing solitude and meditation is that we recover our lives, and perhaps work with God toward restoring His image in us to its rightful place. We cease to be human *doings*; we recover what it means to be human *beings*, and come back in step with the abundant life that Jesus Christ came to reveal. Solitude allows us to grow in our sensitivity both to God and those around us. It is simply not possible to live intentionally for Jesus without habitually ceasing activity and interaction with others, withdrawing into silence, and allowing Christ's Spirit to work within us to renovate our souls to be the places of peace, rest, and contentment we desperately yearn for.

Next we will explore some ways in which we can practically integrate solitude and meditation into our already full lives.

Rediscovering the Practice

The summer that God called me into a life of ministry, I was

---

32. Taken from Thornton Wilder's *Our Town*, 100, as quoted in Don Postema, *Space for God*, 14.

working with Sonshine Ministries—a houseboat-based summer camp on the California River Delta just outside Stockton, California. What an incredible summer that was; waterskiing, worshipping with incredible people, boating and generally loving life. One of the weekly rituals the camp has maintained for more than 25 years was a three-hour solo experience that took place each Thursday morning. Thursday was the last full day of camp and generally a pinnacle of the entire weeklong experience. The solo practice was quite simple; every person, students and adults alike, was to find a place on the island we had anchored to the night prior where they could be alone. Nearly all students, and most adults, had never before spent three hours intentionally alone and were understandably apprehensive. I would give them a few suggestions about what they might want to take with them, various activities they might engage in, and stressed the importance of finding space away from others to focus on God.

Many expressed that they felt like they were being "kicked-off" the houseboat and in to the "wilderness" of the (truly park-like) island. When it came time to begin the solo they would load up sleeping bags, pillows, Bibles, guitars if they brought one, journals, and water bottles. They would then trudge off to some distant part of the island to attempt to be with God. It was not unusual for the campers, and some adults, to begin with a less than optimistic outlook.

However, typically something incredible happened during those hours of alone time. The vast majority of students and adults alike came back on the boat after the entire three hours with significant reports of a strong sense of connection with God. When they reported the things they did (read their Bibles, wrote letters to God, wrote in their journal, sang, prayed, daydreamed, napped, and so on) it was obvious there was nothing spectacular about their activities. The vital ingredient was the amount of time they had and the fact that they were alone seeking to reflect on their lives and their relationship to God.

Each week every participant who came to camp filled out an evaluation about the previous week and their experience. Consistently each week for the 25 years that this camp had been in operation, the solo time received the highest possible marks.

All of us drivers and camp staff absolutely cherished this time each week. After all, when living on a 45' by 12' houseboat for 10 consecutive weeks with anywhere from 11-18 other people, it is quite easy to be overcome by others. This weekly solitude experience provided most of us with the needed alone time to reflect on our relationships with campers and the ministry we'd had that week. It allowed us to make adjustments in our attitudes (if needed) and to finish the week strong—with love toward all. It became such a regular rhythm of our lives that many of us continued the ritual even after camp had ended.

For nearly the entire next year I found myself at a local park in the college town in which I lived, doing my "solo time" on Thursday mornings. God used those weekly meetings with Him to shape me into a different person. He spoke to me in ways I would never have imagined and helped me to reflect meaningfully on my life and walk with Him.

Even today, nearly 15 years later, I attempt to spend solo time with God on a regular basis. Unfortunately, my weekly three-hour solo has become more of an every-six-month occurrence, but still it is a vital part of my life and spiritual journey.

Where to Begin

One of the first steps to take in integrating solitude and mediation into your life is to plan for it to happen. If it is not scheduled, like any other appointment, it will likely never happen. Our lives are often full, and to "find" time just doesn't come about. The time must be intentionally planned. So perhaps if you are persuaded this is a practice that you need to experiment with, the first step in beginning it is to schedule sometime in the next 10 days when you can begin. It is certainly not necessary to spend three hours, but I would suggest at least a whole hour—and frankly more, if you are able. There is something freeing about not looking at your watch because you have such a solid and significant block of time.

Finding a place that you can truly be undisturbed is also helpful. Whether it is a park, in your car (which I did in bad weather), a library, a quiet room in your house and so on, it does not matter much. What matters is that you will have privacy and be alone.

What to do with your time is really up to you. I would suggest taking a Bible or other spiritual reading material (devotional books, autobiographies of important Christians, and so on) along with a journal or laptop. It can be helpful to have some food and water if it will be an extended time alone too. One of the practices I used to love while I was in college was to take a 90-minute hike on a local peak. This time was time for me and God to walk and talk together. I would often get lost in conversation with God—just like He was right there with me. I would have to be careful not to pray/speak too loudly because occasionally I would encounter others on the trail. When this happened they just smiled uncomfortably at me and hurried past.

Final Thoughts

Really there is no "wrong" thing to do in your solitude. With time and practice you will find what works well just for you. It could be some sort of activity like hiking or riding or running, or it may be better for you to simply sit somewhere. What's most important is that your focus and your heart's desire is to connect with God and to use the time to reflect on your life and relationship with Him and others.

If you are apprehensive about this sort of practice, you are not alone. Most people do not spend much time by themselves. Take my word for it; God will meet you in your time of solitude and meditation, just like He has met me.

JOURNALING

By Mickey E Cox

"Journaling blends biblical doctrine and daily living, like the conflu-ence of two great rivers, into one. And since each believer's journey down life's river involves bends and hazards previously unexplored by them . . . something about journaling this journey appeals to the adventuresome spirit of Christian growth." —Donald S. Whitney[33]

The Invitation

YHWH (Hebrew for Yahweh[34], or God, and can also be interpret-ed as Adonai, or Lord) has extended to you an invitation. It's an invi-tation to a conversation about living the God-life. **YHWH**'s been doing this with humankind for some time now. In the past, God has invited people like Abraham, Isaac, Jacob, Moses, David, Esther, and Ruth (the list could go on and on) to this conversation. He has given me this invitation. I'm assuming that if you're reading this chapter then you have interest in accepting His invitation. Considering those familiar biblical names above, it's an honor to think He would invite us to a conversation. So, grab your latte or favorite can of soda, sit down in a comfortable chair, and let's get into His conversation.

Historical Journaling

I've always been intrigued with history, where normal people like you and me shared their stories about life, adventure, and God. For instance, the Hebrew writings describe how the people journeyed together through many adventures—failing sometimes, enduring sometimes, surviving sometimes, and yet often succeed-ing as God's people.

I have studied the journeys of other cultural and ethnic groups and of what made their lives interesting or incredible. I think of what the ancient Greeks and Romans left in their journals and writ-ings that give us a glimpse into what they believed and experienced in everyday life. I also think of what the early Church Fathers wrote

---

33. Whitney, Donald S. *Spiritual Disciplines for the Christian Life* (Colorado Springs: NavPress, 1997), 195.

34. Written Hebrew doesn't have vowels in it.

in their daily journals, which have helped shape past generations' understanding of what living the Christian life is all about. All of these have given us not only insights into their lives and journeys with God, but help us in our own understanding of life. Their writings (or journals) have made a profound difference in our societies today. It is easy to see the importance of journals. Journals are a way for us to chart our journey with God.

When a child is growing up, many parents will have the child stand against a door frame every year and score a notch just above his or her head. As the years pass, those etched-out lines, ever-rising, become so much more than mere scratches in the wood. Each line is a memory, a failure, a triumph, a season of his or her life. Just like looking back into the history of other people in other times, journaling allows us to see where we've been. Behind each jotted word is a picture of God's goodness, mercy, judgment, and power. Each entry holds the developing personality of Christ's love in our lives and, just like notches on a doorframe, helps us to see how far we've come, and how much we've grown.

Journaling

Let's get a good visual picture of the kind of journaling I'm talking about. I'd like for you to clear off your mind's canvas for a minute. Now imagine Indiana Jones sitting at a table by a roaring fire, in some awesome castle, and reading what his father has written in a journal. As you scan the pages, you see a variety of things Indy's dad has scribed that have helped Indiana in his search of fantastic artifacts. The pages include pictures, drawings, quotes, and other information that helped him on his quest. Indy took up his father's story as his own through the journal. Then he carried the adventure on. Can you picture this? This rich imagery may be why we have been so drawn to his movies. We see the adventure he is on, not only through the expedition, but also through what is written on his maps and in his journals. He keeps moving from one adventure to another, never really getting bogged down by anything that would stop him. He keeps traveling, finding new clues and adventures to follow.

Journaling My Journey

The spiritual journey is much the same way. It's about traveling rather than arriving. It's about discovering further rather than about stopping. It's about experiencing all that God has in store, rather than being satisfied with what I have right now. It's about taking time to use what I have learned and experienced then putting that into practice in my life. It's about journeying together with fellow pilgrims. However, sometimes I am in solitude and silence for spiritual growth. This alone time helps me hear what God is revealing to me, and in turn I work through those revelations with others on my journey.

The relationship I have with God may seem at times to have a roller coaster effect. Yet, I don't believe God wants my relationship with Him to be like this over a long stretch of time. He provides me with the tools I need to draw close to Him and to meet with Him everyday. It's much like all of my relationships in life. The more I am with a person, the more I know them by spending time together—eating meals, shopping, sports, music, church services, activities and events. In the middle of our time together, I get to know the other person by talking, sharing, listening, and enjoying his or her company. If I never took time to be with that person, I would not know him or her quite so well, or maybe at all. So it is with God. God loves me immensely and wants to spend time with me everyday. I get to know God through spending time with Him, showing Him I love Him, and expressing my desire to develop this relationship. However, He does challenge me not only to spend time with Him, but to pick up His passion for living the Kingdom life. I demonstrate this passion by getting involved in helping others in their understanding of His Kingdom. Maybe even by serving them at various points. These are the things I write in my journal.

What I'm encouraging you to do now is to go get a journal. You can buy a hardback or spiral journal almost anywhere. You can also make a journal yourself by using a three-ring binder and blank, lined pages. You might even have a Barefoot Ministries *No Limits Discipleship Journal*. If you do, take out all those pages you have read and used, and insert new blank, lined pages.

Now that you have your journal . . .

What I do is write down everything that takes place in my adventures with God. I write in my journal every day, if possible. Some days I might be in a place where it's impossible for me to sit down and write. Yet, when I am consistent about journaling, I feel closer to God. In my closeness, I share all kinds of things with Him in my journal—drawings, poems, quotes, clippings from magazines or articles, and music. It is a recollection of moments in the journey. It reminds me of the things that are influencing me during that time period. My writing is a way of charting where I am spiritually and where I'd like to be that day as a Kingdom member. Also, in my writing time, I will take at least ten minutes to just sit quietly by myself and listen to God. This may be through reading certain scripture passages *(lectio divina)*, listening to some contemplative music, or reading a spiritual formation book. In this silence and solitude, God speaks to me in His still, small voice (I Kings 19:12). I then go back to my journal and write what I believe God has just said to me about my life and my journey with Him. After I've worked in my journal, I can then later chart my progress in the adventure.

I don't think my goal in journaling is to find extremely intuitive insights and thoughts that will be in some amazing book in the future. There are times when I write about what has happened to me in moments of enlightenment. Normally that is not the case, nor my intent. I constantly have to come back to the fact that I am, in my journaling and communication with God, in His presence. Anything that I glean from this daily experience with Him I need to get down on paper so I remember the awesome things God is doing in my life. This comes from allowing Him to work deep in my soul, nurturing it, and changing it to create in me the person He originally intended me to be.

In my journaling practice, or spiritual discipline, I do this not out of duty or obligation, but because I love Him. He's not standing outside my door ready to hit me over the head with a hammer if I don't journal. He won't get mad and punish me if I am not writing. Journaling helps me stay focused; helps me draw closer to God in a manner that assures I won't soon forget what He and I have talked about. So my word to you is, don't let journaling become a problem. Keep the focus on allowing it to be a channel for spiritual growth. Avoid letting it degenerate into just keeping a "rule."

A Word of Advice

When you write on the pages of your journal, remember this rule: be honest with yourself. Take steps in which you can look into your heart and soul; check your feelings, hurts, plans, and struggles with God. When you go through tough times, journaling can help you sort things out on paper, giving you a perspective that is of benefit in your walk with Him. When you go through stress, loss of family or friends, anger, illness, even joy, writing things down in a journal provides a way of processing them that no other means can.

Some Other Ideas

Once you have your journal ready, decide what things might go into your book, other than just writing. You might include things about your spiritual formation stages such as significant pictures you have taken, drawings you have made at a retreat or camp, articles you have come across in your reading, sermon notes, letters of significance or even questions you have not quite got answers to at that time. Literally anything that can be placed in your journal should go there as a reminder later of this time on your journey.

You can also journal prayers. Write down people's names and situations they are going through. Date those so you can look back to see when the request was written and write down when the prayer was answered. However, you might find that the prayer request may not be answered in just the same way you were requesting. God answers all prayers, but in a way that may not resemble your request. You will find that His answers are better in the long run than your request. This will help you understand God more, and the incredible wisdom He has for His creation's well-being.

Use clippings from magazines that prompt you to pray for special situations. These could be pictures of war torn countries, the impoverished, and of marginalized peoples around the world and in your own community. All these will help you focus on maintaining a heart for God and drawing closer to His heartbeat. Be sensitive to how He wants you to develop His compassion in dealing with others.

When you journal, remember to think of it as an ongoing conversation with God. Be open to His leading, as well as what He might be calling you to do in your life right now. You might write down what the Lord is saying to you about your family and their needs. You could write down what the Lord is saying to you about your relationship with some of your friends. You might write down the things He wants you to do to encourage others in their walk with Him. Follow-up these written conversations by writing down the results you experience.

Your journal could reflect some of those conversations with God about what your future might look like as you continue on your journey with Him through high school, college, and beyond. Although I don't think God lays out your future for you to see, I do believe He will talk to you about how He can use you when you offer yourself completely for His Kingdom work.

Final Thoughts

First of all, for quite some time the Church has focused on the assurance of our salvation and "making it to heaven." However, with a clearer understanding of biblical truth, I believe there is more to this life than just the assurance of salvation. Don't misunderstand me and turn to the next chapter. I have a point I want to establish that will make your walk with God more of an adventure. God sent Jesus to reestablish our relationship with Him through His life, passion, death, and resurrection. Jesus died on the Cross and rose again to give us life now and for eternity. It is important to understand that God desires more for our lives than just waiting around to go to heaven. God wants us to live this heavenly life NOW.

Jesus was on earth to show us how God intended for us to live. God calls us to concentrate on our relationship with Him now, and not just focus on "future rewards." The adventure with God begins today, not someday in the future or when we get to heaven! At this very moment I must trust God with my life, and trust Him to mold me into the person He originally created me to be. You and I must allow God to cultivate in us, *now*, what He intends for us to do.

Coming into a right relationship with Him, through Jesus' death and resurrection, is what God is still calling us to do today. Once we accept this restored relationship with God and accept His call to follow Him as His disciple, then we must journey with Him the rest of our lives—here on earth and beyond. It can be summarized in this statement: *"The salvation of our spirit is a miracle in a moment. The journey of a disciple is the task of a lifetime."*

Secondly, it is important to understand that God works in our lives to mold us, form us, and use us to spread His good news here on earth and in our neighborhoods. When Jesus called each of His disciples, He didn't call them to kneel at an altar, sign a commitment card, or sign the back of the four spiritual laws handout. He called them to follow Him—to walk with Him on a journey that took at least three years. Three years of learning how God intended life to be lived here and now. These disciples watched Him as He responded to those who were outcasts and marginalized. They saw the compassion in His eyes as He forgave the adulteress. They noticed how He responded to those who used people. They participated in some incredible miracles that took place right in front of their eyes. They too shared the good news that the Kingdom was near (actually right there around them) and challenged people to turn their lives around and believe. Whether they knew it or not, the disciples were being shaped and formed by the Words and life of Jesus.

We are all in the process of being shaped and formed. We may not always understand that, but it is true. This process can either have a positive or negative effect on our lives. In other words, we can allow ourselves to be shaped into the image of Jesus Christ or into an image that reflects self and the world. Depending on the path we choose, we will either move toward wholeness in Christ or toward a life focused on ourselves. This affects not only our being, but those around us and those people we encounter everyday at home, school, church, work, and so on.

Everything that goes into my mind—every decision I make about life, every action I decide to take, and every feeling or every emotion—has the potential to control me and mold my behavior. This includes my response to the world around me, my relationships, and my reactions toward the people in my life. All these have an effect on me and form me into the person I am becoming.

It becomes clear that I can either become a true disciple of Jesus Christ who is willing to be part of what God wants to do in the world *now*, or I can continue in the absurd unreality and sickness that abounds in the world today.

So, what are you going to do? Are you willing to take this step of faith and move into being formed and molded by God, into the person He originally created you to be? Or do you want to continue in the false lifestyle that the world has to offer? I personally chose to take that step of faith and follow the path of incredible adventure with God! Sometimes it has been the most joyous journey. Sometimes it has been painful when God has asked me to let go of things that hinder my relationship with Him.

Now the invitation to go further on an adventure with God is before you. **If you're willing to do this, then continue in our conversation of how to chart your adventure through journaling.** I believe the result will be Christian spiritual formation. (Christian spiritual formation happens when we allow the transformation process to occur in us as a disciple of Jesus Christ *now*, so that we may tell God's story through our lives.)

I could go on and give you many more examples, thoughts, and ideas about journaling. The main thing right now is for you to keep it simple and make it your own by just starting to journal. As time progresses and you find yourself further down the road on this journey with God, you can begin branching out and creating even more extensive journals. For now, to simply begin is the important thing. May God be especially near as you begin charting your adventure with Him!

For Further Reading

A Spiritual Formation Journal by Jana Rea. (HarperSanFrancisco Publishing)

Celebration of Discipline by Richard Foster. (HarperSanFrancisco Publishing)

Journal Keeping by Luann Budd. (InterVarsity Press)

Living the Mission: A Spiritual Formation Guide by Lynda L. Graybeal and Julia L. Roller. (HarperSanFrancisco Publishing)

Simplify Your Spiritual Life by Donald S. Whitney. (NavPress)

Spending Time With God by Mark Gilroy. (Beacon Hill Press of Kansas City)

Spiritual Disciplines for the Christian Life by Donald S. Whitney. (NavPress)

Spiritual Disciplines Handbook by Adele Ahlberg Calhoun. (InterVarsity Press)

CONFESSION

By Brooklyn Lindsey

"Confess your sins to each other and pray for each other so that you may be healed" (James 5:16).

I had writer's block writing this chapter for *Sacred Life*. I sat staring at my computer toggling back and forth from *iTunes* to *facebook*. I was searching for something to spark the mental treadmill and give me some insight, some golden nugget of wisdom that would set me in the right direction. My hope was to begin to understand in some small way the value of confession and why it might be important for a young person to begin this practice now rather than later. As I searched and felt various degrees of panic when nothing surfaced, I began to wonder if I was looking in the wrong places. So I stopped looking for something new or remarkably profound and asked a simple question: why do we need confession?

I need confession. Why? Because there is something freeing in letting it all out. When someone else knows me as I truly am and hears my confessions, they see what makes me human. Pride drips away and we find solidarity as we walk together in a journey that isn't always easy. Sharing my struggles (my real struggles) with sin is one of the most difficult and rewarding things I can do. There are only a few people that earn this type of open friendship, but it's something I would willingly trade many surface friendships for because they make me stronger. They help me grow.

So what does it mean to enter into a lifestyle of confession? We can begin by understanding that confession is given to us as a gift that can heal us, an agent that can cleanse our conscience and give us strength. Confession is a biblical act of obedience and has been practiced by the Church for thousands of years. However, even with its promise of healing, I tend to neglect it in my daily walk with Christ. Many of you are probably the same. Confession lays dormant within, covered up under blankets of fear and doubt. I've also neglected the spiritual discipline of confession because of the common reasoning that "I'm not Catholic." I'm learning that confession isn't something one church owns as their trademark. It's a way of life that every Christian can embrace and benefit from. Confession is universal. It's something that transcends church doctrine, and it's a practice that anyone can embrace regardless of theological upbringing.

In this chapter, we'll take a brief look at the history of confession and its beginnings in the Catholic Church, how it has changed, and how it might benefit a postmodern teenager. I'll discuss some ways confession can become embedded in your daily life with God. Confession, no matter how muddled it has become in its expression in the modern world, is a habit that holds power to change our lives.

If we could go back in time and spy on the Early Church, we might be surprised to see people openly confessing their sins to each other in public. The New Testament scriptures never really describe confession as a formal act, but it does encourage it. In James 5:16 we read the most classic example of the body of Christ being encouraged to confess their sins openly to one another. 1 John 1:9 talks about the power of confession to God: *"If we confess our sins he is faithful and just and will forgive us our sins and purify us from all unrighteousness."* James 5:16 sheds light on the role confession plays within the body of Christ. He writes that the church should confess their sins to one another and to pray for one another. Confession was a habit made by those already believing in Christ, who sought forgiveness for their sins.

Confession to God, confession to ourselves, and confession to others is a model that comes straight from the New Testament scriptures. Its expression in our world has changed so much over time that it proves important to go back and discover why we began formal confession in the first place.

Confession within certain parts of the Church progressed and became a formal act when an Irish monk, the abbot of Luxeuil, introduced confession to the church people. As congregations were exposed to the practice of clergy-to-clergy confession, they started warming up to the idea of personal confession to the priest.[35] A group of clergy met together in 1215 at The Lateran Council and made regular confession an absolute law of the

35. Jackson, Samuel Macauley. *Schaff-Herzog Encyclopedia of Religious Knowledge* (Grand Rapids: Baker Book House, 1952), 221.

Roman Catholic Church. This was followed by the requirement for Christians to confess once a year, receive communion at least at Easter, and faithfully and privately acknowledge all sins. The words "I absolve thee" became judicial words spoken by clergy, and believers began relying on the verbal granting of pardon by the priest for sins. Also, the practice of selling "indulgences" by the priest was introduced. That is, when someone confessed their sin, they were granted relief from the suffering awaiting them in purgatory. This meant that if someone sinned, they could confess and pay money; thereby being forgiven and released from punishment in the afterlife. This "selling" turned into a way for the clergy to make money off of those seeking forgiveness through confession.

During the Middle Ages, some parts of Italy, Europe, France, and Germany adopted a more general approach to confession. A confession would be read in a church service, in front of the people, and absolution would be received as a body. Overall, there was opposition to the confessional system instituted by church leaders, and some people resisted the ways it was being forced upon believers.

Martin Luther was one who disagreed with the system most openly. He believed it had turned into a way for priests (or the church) to make money as they sold and granted forgiveness. Something that was meant to be free, a gift offered to all people regardless of financial status, was being bought and sold in the church. Luther also felt that this type of confession was a torture to the conscience. It was something that no believer should be made to endure. He didn't reject confession, only the ways it was being used to oppress people in the church. Luther stood firm on the truth that forgiveness could be received without the priest or clergy offering it. It could be done through Christ alone.

Confession has a come a long way since the days of the Early Church. Today, in our postmodern context, confession has lost some of its original purpose. What was created for the repentant sinner has, in some ways, been commercialized and misunderstood. Confession is a powerful and biblical ritual that, if given a chance, could revolutionize our spiritual lives. First and foremost, confession is most powerful when confessing our sin(s) before God. This is where we come to God and admit we need His mercy, grace, and forgiveness in our lives. Think about the Psalmist's words:

"Blessed are those who transgressions are forgiven, whose sins are cov-

ered. Blessed are those whose sin the LORD does not count against them and in whose spirit is no deceit. When I kept silent, my bones wasted away through my groaning all day long . . . then I acknowledged my sin to you and did not cover up my iniquity. I said, "I will confess my transgression to the LORD." And you forgave the guilt of my sin. Therefore let all the faithful pray to you while you may be found; surely the rising of the mighty waters will not reach them" (Psalm 32:1-6, TNIV).

If we return to the book of James, we'll find this letter to the church voices concern that everyone should confess their sins to one another and pray for each other (5:16). Think about how this helps us. One writer puts it this way,

"James advises the mutual confession of sins. This practice involves a process of self-criticism and personal and communal purification. It requires enough humility to bow our heads and let another pray for us. It means honesty and the confession of personal and collective sins, without fear, with the freedom of love. It means opening ourselves to God in silent prayer. The community that accepts this challenge will enter into the deep process of integrity to which it is invited."[36]

This type of confession has the potential to liberate us all from feeling the weight and loneliness of sin.

How often do we freak out or become judgmental in our hearts when a brother or sister in Christ is discovered to be involved in sin? We all have sinned and have come short of God's glory (Romans 3:23), but it's so easy to forget this truth. When we hold our sins secret in "pious fellowship"[37] and never confess them to God and to each other, we feel alone and ashamed. It's important to have fellowship together as Christian people, forgiven and growing in grace. It is also important to have fellowship as those who are tempted and sometimes fall, knowing and sharing our burdens in the community of faith.

Dietrich Bonhoeffer explains how sin keeps us from confessing. Confession is the breakthrough to community.

"Sin demands to have a man [woman] *by himself* [herself]. *It withdraws* [a person] *from the community. The more isolated a person is, the more destructive will be the power of sin over him* [her], *and the more deeply*

---

36. Tamez, Elsa. *The Scandalous Message of James: Faith Without Works Is Dead* (New York: The Crossroad Publishing Company, 1985), 59.

37. Bonhoeffer, Dietrich. *Life Together* (San Francisco: Harper Collins, 1954), 110.

he [she] *becomes involved in it, the more disastrous is his [her] isolation. Sin wants to remain unknown."*[38]

In confession, there is also a breakthrough to the Cross. The root of sin, pride, must be overcome in order to tell someone else our struggles.

"Confession in the presence of a brother [or sister] is the profoundest kind of humiliation. It hurts . . . it is a dreadful blow to pride . . . it is nothing else but our fellowship with Jesus Christ that leads us to the dying that comes in confession, in order that we may in truth share the Cross. The Cross of Jesus Christ destroys all pride."[39]

When we confess, a breakthrough to new life occurs. I didn't understand this as a child. In fact, I was afraid of confession more than anything. Have you ever tried to confess everything you've ever done wrong in thirty seconds? Thirty seconds is the amount of time I had to pray and confess between the pastor's communion words and the actual eating and drinking of the elements. It's an impossible task to confess everything in and of itself, let alone in such a short amount of time. Still, my childhood ideas about confession led me to think that it was necessary to urgently seek forgiveness in church for anything that might be deemed unworthy in my life. I can still hear my grandfather telling me at a very young age that Communion is sacred and that the Bible tells us not to drink from the cup in an unworthy way. Unworthy in a child's mind could mean anything. Confession became a regular part of my prayer life from then on. Fear would grip my heart if the Communion elements came down the aisle unannounced (like while I had been napping during the sermon), then I would use the back-up prayer "Lord, forgive me for EVERYTHING, I'm so sorry." Since my childhood, I've grown in many ways spiritually. However, there are still times that my very narrow understanding of confession peaks its way into my life again.

Bonhoeffer says, *"Where sin is hated, admitted, and forgiven, there the break with the past is made . . . confession is conversion. 'Behold, all things become new.'" (II Cor. 5:17) Christ has made a new beginning with us."*[40] In confession, we can break away from self-deception. Our brothers and sisters in Christ help us minimize our blind spots to

---

38. Ibid., 114.
39. Ibid., 115.
40. Ibid., 115.

see ourselves as we truly are, sinners saved by grace. Bonhoeffer also says, *"A [person] who confesses his [her] sins in the presence of a brother [or sister] knows that he [she] is no longer alone with himself [herself], he [she] experiences the reality of God in the other person. As long as I am by myself in the confession of my sins everything remains in the dark, but in the presence of a brother the sin has to be brought into the light . . . it is better that it happens today between me and my brother, rather than on the last day in the piercing light of the final judgment. It is a mercy that we can confess our sins to a brother."*[41]

One of the most intriguing forms of confession I've seen in the past few years was in the book *Post Secret* by Frank Warren. *Post Secret* has become an ongoing community art project where people mail in their secrets anonymously on one side of a homemade postcard. The anonymous postcards are decorated to spell out a secret they've never told anyone before. The confessions that come in are astounding, absurd, disturbing, and some are ridiculously funny. Warren was able to bring unity to a group of strangers who confessed on the pages of his book those things they couldn't speak in public. I found it fascinating and even hopeful, because if the secular world can see the value of public confession and its cleansing and healing nature, perhaps our Christian community could take confession one step further. That is, to see confession as a way to heal us of our past and present struggles.

How can we access the freedom and encouragement that comes from "confessing our sins to one another"? Who, in our fast-paced, competitive, don't-make-a-mistake-or-it-will-ruin-you world, would dare confess their sins to another person?

Let's take a look at the story of the lost and wandering son in Luke 15:11-31. We see the story of a young man wanting independence from his father and a desire to make a life of his own. His father's wisdom was greater than his own, but he insisted on collecting his inheritance early and making his own way. Luke tells us of the son's downward spiral into a dark place of wandering and purposelessness. After all of his money was gone and all of his options were exhausted, the son finds himself homeless and begging for food.

The work of the Lord in the son's life occurs when he doesn't allow pride to block him from moving towards his father in confes-

---

41. Ibid., 116.

sion. There was no way for him to go home proud. He had ruined and squandered everything. His going home was admittance that he couldn't make it on his own, that his father was right, and that he needed help. How many of us need to return to God in confession for the way we have wandered and ruined the gifts that have been given to us? Confession strips away our pride and helps us to be loved fully by a forgiving and just God.

Confession can be practiced as a spiritual discipline in many ways. There's no prescribed method or mandated way of confession. It's a discipline that God desires for us to grow into. Each of you should consider how it might have a place in your daily walk with the Lord.

Here are some different paths to the discipline of confession.

Journaling

Writing prayers of confession to God is a good way to begin your discipline of confession. At first you may not be comfortable confessing your sins to someone else. Begin by opening up your heart to God. Allow God to mold you and shape you as you reflect on those things that you give to Jesus in prayer. As I look back on journal entries from my teenage years, I see many moments of confession; moments when I felt I had no one else to turn to but the pages of a notebook. I found relief in letting my burdens become known to God through written prayer. Journaling also helps us connect with lessons of the past, and to see progress as we grow.

Accountability Friendships

My first encounter with the idea of having an "accountability partner" came at an Acquire the Fire event. The speaker at the event shared the importance of having an "in your face" friend. I never forgot that phrase and it helped me seek genuine friendships. The Bible says that a cord of three strands is hard to break (Ecclesiastes 4:12). We are stronger together. Having a friend you can trust enough to keep you straight is a priceless gift. We are stronger when we are able to ask each other the hard questions and able to confess our weak areas so that we can figure out how God can work to mature us in these situations.

Altar Prayer

Many churches still use altars or kneeling benches as places to pray. Altar workers or prayer partners may or may not know you, but they are there to hear your requests and pray on your behalf. God uses the Holy Spirit to convict our hearts of sin. Paying attention to your heart when it seems filled with a godly sorrow is something that might lead you to pray at an altar or to a time of confession. The next time your youth pastor or church leader offers an invitation to go forward physically to pray, think about how you might be able to use that time to confess temptation or areas of sin. Sometimes we get intimidated about what others might think when we go to pray. Remember, we all have fallen short of God's glory and we are all growing. Don't be afraid to join with other believers as you grow in the Lord and set an example for others to follow (1 Timothy 4:12).

Mentor or Spiritual Director

Some of my biggest growth experiences have happened as a result of serious confession conversations. Friends or leaders who understand the complexities of humanity can enter into dialogue that sheds light on our blind spots. Having someone you can trust to see the areas you may overlook is really valuable and helpful. They can see the things that really hurt us, our relationships, and our commitment to God. We have to be open to giving and receiving in this type of relationship, but the benefits are eternal.

In the Catholic tradition confessors, sometimes priests or other spiritual directors, are the people a confessing sinner shares their burdens with. Confessors hear the confession and help the confessing person turn their heart and minds toward repentance. In the holiness church we believe that a person can be sanctified, or cleansed from the willful longing to sin against God. A confessor for us is someone we can confide in with our struggle to overcome our sin nature. It can be any person that edifies and challenges us to grow to be more like Christ.

Communion

Communion is a memorial to the death and passion of Christ. It is a ritual for all who have true repentance for their sins and who believe in the Lord for their salvation. This ritual allows us to draw near to God and become participants in Christ's redeeming sacrifice. As we remember and sit at the table of the Lord together, we are reminded that we are all seeking in true humility and faith, for-giveness and transformation. Confession has been a way of life that develops for me as I am given opportunity to remember Christ in Communion more often. Find out when your church shares the sacrament of Communion and make time to experience the rewards of confession and remembrance.

Final Thoughts

In a short while, my first book will be published and available to the public. It's ironic that its title includes the word "confes-sions." I loved writing the book. It's a reflection of me, my hang-ups, and quirks (precisely the things that make me nervous about other people reading it). The danger in confession is that it opens us up to be vulnerable to others, but this is so important. Confession makes us real. It requires risk because we could be judged. But what I've learned during this process of writing the book is that God defines who we are and gives us worth. The more transparent I become, the more I am able to relate to others who are also struggling. We make room for others when we live in this way. We offer hospitality to real people with real issues. Confession removes our masks and unites us as seekers. Developing a lifestyle of confession can only lead us to a better understanding of what it truly means to love and be loved both in our relationship with God and in our relationship with others.

PILGRIMAGES

By Mike King

"Blessed are those whose strength is in you, who have set their hearts on pilgrimage" (Psalm 84:5).

I had a great childhood. I was blessed with great parents, siblings, friends, and lived in a wonderful community. My memories of growing up are almost entirely positive. However, when I reminisce on the childhood experiences that are powerfully imbedded in my memory and recall the most vivid and shaping events that happened to me as a child, I'm amazed at how many of them occurred while on a trip or vacation. I remember our first family vacation in Colorado. I was overwhelmed, even as young as I was, by the beauty of the Rocky Mountains. The majestic waterfalls and the cold, clear, powerful mountain streams, mystical caves, and unique rock formations all added to the magic of the experience. Even as a young child I remember feeling enthusiastically alive and spiritual. During early adolescence, I remember a trip to the East Coast where I saw the Atlantic Ocean for the first time. Seeing the ocean had the same effect on me as being in the mountains of Colorado. I was besieged with a sense of awe.

At the age of twenty-two I made my first trip out of the country. During this trip I visited Rome, Italy, and Israel. Wow. This experience, which I would come to understand later as a pilgrimage, had a profound impact on my life. I knew in my heart that I would be doing this again. I decided to make this a part of my rhythm of life and spiritual formation. I also knew that I wanted others in my life to experience what I had experienced. I'm actually writing part of this chapter while in the Middle East (my 21st Pilgrimage). During these 21 trips, I have taken more than 400 people, mostly young people, to experience a pilgrimage in the lands of the Bible. For nearly two thousand years our Christian family members have practiced pilgrimage for the purpose of growth, discovery, learning, and to nurture their spiritual formation.

We find the earliest semblance of pilgrimage showing up in the Old Testament when Abraham and Sarah were called to embark

sacred
life

on a journey with God to a land of promise. The concept of pilgrimage was woven into the spirituality of Old Testament believers. Psalms 120 through 134 were written specifically for the purpose of being sung by pilgrims on the way to Jerusalem and the Temple. Jesus and His family made several pilgrimages to Jerusalem, as did all good Jewish families living in the Middle East during that time. The account of Jesus being found by His parents in the Temple, confounding the scholars with His wisdom, occurred when Jesus was accidentally left behind in Jerusalem during a pilgrimage.

Pilgrimage continued to play a key role in the life of the Early Church. Origen, a 3rd century church father, said that followers of Jesus must walk with passion in the "footsteps of Christ, of the Prophets, and of the Apostles." From the earliest days of the new Christian Church, pilgrimage has been practiced as a way to emphasize a connection of the internal journey of the heart with an external physical journey of discovery and growth. The earliest pilgrimages were a way to take up the *"via cruces"* (the way of the cross, the way of crucifixion). The destination of these ancient pilgrimages were primarily the places connected to Jesus—His birth place, the places He taught and did miracles, His place of crucifixion, burial, resurrection, and ascension. A pilgrimage was a way to reenact and embrace the way of Jesus. Jesus not only left His place in heaven to become a human being, but a human being who had no place to lay His head. Jesus was on the road, on a journey, and on a mission. Pilgrims were invited to follow Jesus on this journey and mission. The pilgrim willingly left his or her comfort zone for time spent in spiritual discovery and enlightenment. Yet, pilgrims who left their normal environments for a period of time eventually returned to their normal environments. The goal was to return home from the journey and pilgrimage with a sense that they had taken a significant step forward in their spiritual development. The concept of pilgrimage in early Christianity became firmly established and widely accepted as a metaphor for salvation and the spiritual journey.

Pilgrimage was further formalized and broadly valued as an important aspect of Christian formation as early as the beginning of the medieval period. Many early Church documents referred to the importance of making pilgrimage to holy places. Several of these manuscripts claim that the tradition of pilgrimage emerged in the days of the Apostles. Interestingly, we find in many ancient writings words of critique and caution about pilgrimage possibly having negative results. Why? Some were trying to capitalize on the popularity of pilgrimage by taking advantage of pilgrims. It seems that pilgrimage was being organized into a lucrative business as early as the 5th and 6th centuries. In order to provide direction for the early pilgrims, several early theologians and ministry leaders emphasized to followers of Jesus that one could as easily encounter the Presence of God in their homes, communities, and places of worship as they could if they traveled to some far-off, exotic location. Prolific Christian leaders and theologians such as St. Augustine and Jerome reminded followers of Jesus that pilgrimage was not essential or necessary to encounter God.

In some church periods pilgrimage was linked to a penitent pursuit and purpose—a journey to deal with the sinfulness of the pilgrim and to seek peace with oneself and with God. Most of the time the target of the pilgrimage was to trace the steps and activities of saints or other important people and events. The practice of pilgrimage, in some form, is nearly universal. There seems to be something naturally in the hearts of human beings that encourages the desire to pursue pilgrimage. We see some manner of pilgrimage in every culture and religion throughout the world.

So what does the current spiritual practice of pilgrimage look like for you? Reminisce for awhile. What formative experiences have you had? Why were these experiences so memorable? As I gradually recognized a pattern of God using the experience of travel to profoundly shape me spiritually, I became intentional about pursuing the practice of pilgrimage. I also deliberately embraced the metaphor of pilgrimage as a lifelong journey with God in the way of Jesus Christ. How might you embrace pilgrimage as a part of your spirituality and formation?

I admit that I was quite fortunate to have the opportunity to make a pilgrimage to the Middle East at a young age. Maybe you haven't had this opportunity, yet. However, many of you reading this have probably been involved in some kind of short-term mission experience. If you were, it was most likely something that impacted you deeply. I believe that it would probably be more accurate to call "youth mission trips," "youth pilgrimages." Most of the time it seems the mission trip has a greater impact on the participants of the team than the people being targeted. This should not be dismissed as unimportant. If the idea of pilgrimage was incorporated into the mission trip, I think there would be better overall results for all involved. If you haven't been on a short-term mission trip, maybe you can recall a retreat you experienced with your youth group or an amazing week of summer camp. All of these experiences have in common the dynamic of "displacement" at work in us. Displacement, in its simple form, involves the act of getting out of your normal environment. Being out of our regular routines and comfort zone heightens our awareness of what is happening to us and around us. During these times, and in these environments, we may be more likely to recognize the ministry of the Holy Spirit in our lives.

Perhaps you sense that pilgrimage as a spiritual practice is something you would like to explore. How do you get started? Begin praying for the Holy Spirit to speak to you and give you ideas. Study your upcoming schedule and consider setting aside a time period—a long weekend, a spring break or a summer vacation—for a possible pilgrimage. Is this something you want to do alone, with friends, or perhaps a small group at church? I would suggest establishing a regular time to pray and listen for specific ideas that God may impress upon your heart and mind concerning what a pilgrimage might look like for you. Pray about possible companions to experience this with you. Pray about potential destinations for your pilgrimage. The first pilgrimage you intentionally plan doesn't have to be a month-long journey to a far-off land. Perhaps a weekend pilgrimage that is easy to plan is a good way to get started. I have done many one day and weekend pilgrimages.

A couple of years ago I discovered that I had an entire Saturday with my family out of town, and I had nothing on my schedule. I decided that I would visit the places that were a significant part of my childhood. I live relatively close to where I grew up, so I traveled less than 50 miles during this one day mini-pilgrimage. Even so, this experience was amazing. I visited the home that I lived in from the age of five to eighteen. My childhood home appeared to be so much smaller than I thought it was as a ten-year-old. I reminisced about the times I had played baseball in a variety of neighborhood makeshift fields. The woods that I used to explore were no longer intimidating as they were when I was twelve years old. I had a wonderful one-hour conversation with the parents of my childhood best friend. I visited my elementary school and relived classic kickball games and incidents that had occurred on the playground. I remembered the locations of my classes. I drove around the neighborhood remembering the homes of friends. I retraced my old paper route—it sure didn't seem like it could have been as hard of a route as I had remembered. I saw the place where I held a girl's hand for the first time. I lingered at places that were favorite adolescent hangouts. I drove by my junior high school and loitered in the parking lot of my high school.

While most of the memories I had that day were pleasant, there were other thoughts which made me sad or raised issues for me to reckon with. A mini-pilgrimage that I thought might take half a morning turned into an all day and evening experience. During this day of discovery, other places and experiences continually surfaced for me to add to the agenda. I felt the presence of the Holy Spirit throughout the day. I remembered. I was filled with gratitude. Many times throughout the day I learned more about myself. Often I found myself smiling and a few times I was filled with sadness and deep emotion. I ate at one of my favorite eating establishment that hadn't changed in 35 years. I ordered the same meal I ordered as a sixteen-year-old. I appreciated my parents and siblings. My heart was filled with thankfulness toward God and I wondered how different my life would be now if certain events hadn't happened. By the end of the day I felt fully alive and grounded deeply in the life of God. What a day this was. The total cost for this day was less than 25 dollars, but the results were invaluable.

Returning to a place where you had previously experienced a spiritual awakening or a profound encounter with God is another idea to build a pilgrimage around. There is a spot at YouthFront Camp where the Holy Spirit spoke to me as a 19-year-old kid. When I return to that spot it is easy to remember the freshness of that experience. There is a location where I met with God often near a cabin at the Lake of the Ozarks. This place brings back rich memories of great spiritual depth. I have made 21 pilgrimages to the land of the Bible. All the emotion and memories of times spent in prayer at The Sea of Galilee, Jerusalem, and The Empty Tomb in Israel flow easily in my thoughts and resurface every time I revisit those places. Amazing experiences and memories at the Maritine Prison of Paul in Rome; Berchtesgarden in the Bavarian Alps; the Conception Abbey north of my home in Kansas City; and the Prayer Chapel at YouthFront Camp all come easily flooding back when I reminisce how God met me in those places. All of these locations have become "sacred spaces" for me because I encountered God there in special ways. God often meets His people in such unique ways that the location of the encounter becomes a memorial and symbol of God's work in our life.

We see an example of this in the life of Abraham, the father of our faith. In the 12th chapter of Genesis, God called Abram to leave his country and go to a land that God would show him. When he arrived in Canaan, the Lord appeared to him. Abram built an altar and worshipped the Lord. This location became a special place—a place where Abram met and communed with God. It would become a place for future pilgrimage.

"The LORD appeared to Abram and said, 'To your offspring I will give this land.' So he built an altar there to the LORD, who had appeared to him. From there he went on toward the hills east of Bethel and pitched his tent, with Bethel on the west and Ai on the east. There he built an altar to the LORD and called on the name of the LORD" (Genesis 12:7, 8).

After this great experience of encountering the Presence of God, Abram went to Egypt, where he got into some challenging situations. Abram left Egypt and was compelled to return to Bethel, the place in which he had so powerfully encountered the Presence of God.

"Abram had become very wealthy in livestock and in silver and gold. From the Negev he went from place to place until he came to Bethel, to the place between Bethel and Ai where his tent had been earlier and where he had first built an altar. There Abram called on the name of the LORD" (Genesis 13:2-4).

Abram, whose name was changed by God to Abraham, undoubtedly spoke to his children about experiencing the Presence of God and how God met with him at Bethel. Later, Abraham's grandson Jacob was on a pilgrimage and had an encounter with the Presence of God. Jacob was sleeping and had a dream in which the Lord God appeared to him.

"When Jacob awoke from his sleep, he thought, 'Surely the LORD is in this place, and I was not aware of it.' He was afraid and said, 'How awesome is this place! This is none other than the house of God; this is the gate of heaven.' Early the next morning Jacob took the stone he had placed under his head and set it up as a pillar and poured oil on top of it. He called that place Bethel" (Genesis 28:16-19).

Many years later Jacob found himself in a very stressful situation with his father-in-law, Laban. God appeared to him again in a dream and said,

"I am the God of Bethel, where you anointed a pillar and where you made a vow to me. Now leave this land at once and go back to your native land" (Genesis 31:13).

After Jacob resettled in the land of his birth, he, like his father, found himself in challenging life situations. Seeking help, Jacob heard again from God.

"Then God said to Jacob, 'Go up to Bethel and settle there, and build an altar there to God, who appeared to you when you were fleeing from your brother Esau'" (Genesis 35:1).

Jacob sensed that he was coming once again to this sacred space where he would encounter the Presence of God and had all the idols purged from his family's belongings. Jacob prepared to meet God. When Jacob came into the Presence of God, he was told that his name was to change from Jacob to Israel. God then made Israel a promise.

"'The land I gave to Abraham and Isaac I also give to you, and I will give this land to your descendants after you.' Then God went up from him at the place where he had talked with him. Jacob set up a stone pillar at the place where God had talked with him, and he poured out a drink offering on it; he also poured oil on it. Jacob called the place where God had talked with him Bethel" (Genesis 35:12-15).

Jesus called His followers to leave their homes, their families, and their possessions. There was a significant cost involved in following Jesus. His disciples had to be willing to leave the lives they knew. They were displaced from their normal environment in order to learn what it would mean for them to pick up their cross and follow Jesus. Luke writes, *"As they were walking along the road, a man said to him, 'I will follow you wherever you go.' Jesus replied, 'Foxes have holes and birds of the air have nests, but the Son of Man has no place to lay his head.' He said to another man, 'Follow me.' But the man replied, 'Lord, first let me go and bury my father.' Jesus said to him, 'Let the dead bury their own dead, but you go and proclaim the kingdom of God.' Still another said, 'I will follow you, Lord; but first let me go back and say good-by to my family.' Jesus replied, 'No one who puts his hand to the plow and looks back is fit for service in the kingdom of God'"* (Luke 9:57-62).

Pilgrimage enables us to embark on a journey of faith and discovery that can be deeply transformational. In the Early Church, the leaders of the community were poor and often forced to wander without the security of a stable life and home. The apostle Paul traveled all over the ancient Roman Empire for the purpose of spreading the Good News of Jesus Christ. Paul had to depend on God to provide for him. He never knew what tomorrow would bring. Pilgrimage allows us to identify with the apostles, early Church leaders, and pilgrims of old.

Final Thoughts

Pilgrimages have played a significant role in my spiritual development. As a part of my *"rhythm of life,"* I desire to make at least one pilgrimage per year. I know that this is not practical for many people. Perhaps a pilgrimage once every three or five years is more achievable.

In addition to the most common pilgrimage destinations connected to biblical places (i.e.; Israel, Palestine, Rome, Greece, Egypt, Jordan, and Turkey), here are some other pilgrimage ideas:

- Santiago de Compostela in northwestern Spain where James, the disciple of Jesus, is believed to be buried.
- Iona (an island off the west coast of Scotland) where the Celtic missionary St. Columba built a monastery in the 6th century.
- Canterbury in England, where Thomas Becket the Archbishop of Canterbury was martyred. This pilgrimage site was popularized by Chaucer's *Canterbury Tales*.
- Ireland for me is one big Pilgrimage site with historic places like Glendalough and Clonmacnois.

- ❧ Taize is a prayer community in the south of France near Lyon. Every week during the summer, thousands of young people come to spend a week in prayer at this unique place.
- ❧ Assisi, Italy where St. Francis established his ministry and religious order.
- ❧ Wittenberg, Germany where Martin Luther launched the Reformation.
- ❧ London, Epworth, Oxford, Bristol and other places associated with the life of John Wesley.

We do not take a pilgrimage for the purpose of arriving at a new destination of spiritual enlightenment. We embrace the concept of pilgrimage to lean into the reality that we are on a lifelong journey with the Holy Spirit—who is our guide and teaches us how to discover full life with God in the way of Jesus Christ. Pilgrimage helps us synthesize our inward journey with our outward journey. May our Lord Jesus Christ bless you and keep you faithfully on your pilgrimage throughout your entire life.

IMAGO DEI

By Brooklyn Lindsey

"So God created human beings in his own image, in the image of God he created them; male and female he created them" (Genesis 1:27, TNIV).

The moment of our daughters' birth stands in memory as one of the most beautiful and transformative events in my life. Hearing her cry and seeing her tiny form created waves of compassion and love for someone that I had just met for the first time. In that precious and sacred moment, my husband and I fell in love with Kirra who, ironically, looked nothing like us. When Kirra was born she had coal black hair (tons of it), a red face, smashed nose, puffy eyes, and very dark skin. Most babies come into the world like this. Their Yoda-like resemblance is nothing to be worried about, and changes within hours of birth. As the days pass, Kirra grows to look more like us. Our features are infused in her DNA and it's funny to see new strands develop daily. Now that Kirra is ten months old, she is beginning to look like us more and more. She bears the image of her birth parents and we have great joy seeing ourselves mirrored in her.

We too have been given a spiritual parent. Discovering the image of our Creator-Parent can inform our past and help us look toward the future. I think of the closure some adopted children receive when they learn of their birth parents. Even if the person came from unfortunate circumstances, there is something liberating in knowing where he or she came from. It is the same with God. God breathed into the first human, giving them life. He breathes into each one of us, giving us life and purpose. But like our earthly parents, it takes time to understand what bearing an image truly means. When a child is born, he or she resembles the parents. When an animal is born to a species, it resembles the species and not some other group of animals. Yet, the *imago dei* (the image of God) is much more than species identification. It is a biblical concept that has a great spiritual impact on our lives.

The image of God, or *imago dei*, in humanity has been a subject of varied understanding. It might be easy for someone to overlook this central belief of the Church because of its complexities and move on to something not as difficult to comprehend. However, an understanding of the *imago dei* is central to the Christian's response to the Creator. Therefore, the idea that we are created in the image of the God is something we as humans must come to understand. How we understand ourselves to be created in God's own image affects our response to the Creator and our path toward restoration.

Imago Dei: Old Testament

"The Old Testament teaching regarding the image of God places its focus upon [human]'s likeness to God in abilities, especially the ability of dominion . . .the image is not primarily described in terms of moral righteousness . . . but in the exercising of dominion over the earth . . . "[42]

The two narratives in Genesis 1 and 2 affirm that we are created from the earth, together with the animals of the field and the birds of the air. However, we have been created uniquely. Genesis 1 says that God created humankind in His image: *"'Let us make humankind in our image, according to our likeness; and let them have dominion over the fish of the sea, and over the birds of the air, and over the cattle, and over all the wild animals of the earth, and over every creeping thing that creeps upon the earth.' So God created humankind in his image, in the image of God he created them; male and female he created them"* (Genesis 1:26-27, NRSV). God did not create anything, other than humans, with His image stamped upon their being. We were created to bear the image of our Maker, something nothing else God created can claim.

What does it mean to be created in God's image? This means that God *"placed within each person the capacity for deep love for Him and deep godly love for each person."*[43] We were created to have relationship with God and to reflect His likeness in our heart and lives. Unfortunately, when Adam and Eve sinned, this image was damaged. God gave them a choice to obey, but their self-centeredness bent them toward their own will, rather than God's will. The result of Adam and Eve's sin was their descendents (anyone who has ever lived since these two people) would be born with this inclination to reflect their own image, instead of reflecting their Creator's.

42. Cubie, David L. *Into His Likeness: Various Papers on the Doctrine of Entire Sanctification* (Mount Vernon Nazarene College, 1980), 17.

43. Kipp, Mike and Wade, Kenny. *Being Real* (Kansas City: Barefoot Ministries, 2007), 36.

Imago Dei: New Testament

"The Son is the image of the invisible God, the firstborn over all creation" (Colossians 1:15, TNIV).

When Adam and Eve sinned, the perfect fellowship between humankind and God was broken. Sin entered the world and humankind's tendency was to live for self. Since that time, humans have been inclined to mimic each other instead of trying to emulate the ways of God. *"Instead of reflecting God, we reflect one another. John's Gospel describes the Jewish authorities as loving 'the praise of men rather than the praise of God'"* (John 12:43).[44] This is a life struggle! As we live, we look to others for approval, value, and acceptance, when all along God is waiting to give us all of these things when we seek His ways.

When Christ came, His life and actions were the reflection of God to all the earth. Everything Jesus did was to show us who the Heavenly Father was. When Christ died on the Cross and shed His blood, reconciliation between God and humankind was made possible. Colossians 1:19-20 says, *"For God was pleased to have all his fullness dwell in him, and through him to reconcile earth or things in heaven, by making peace through his blood, shed on the Cross."* When we become followers of Christ, God begins to restore His image within us by the power of the Holy Spirit. Frank Moore says that *"when we return to God and surrender our self-will to Him, He restores our moral image as a prisoner regaining freedom after serving a prison term."*[45] As Christians following in the footsteps of Christ, the image of God is reflected in our hearts and lives. Through Christ and the power of the Holy Spirit, the image of God is being restored in us as we live in daily relationship with Him.

Imago Dei: John Wesley

John Wesley offers another way of thinking about the *imago dei*, through the means of grace. The means of grace "are ways God helps people grow as Christians."[46] Some of these *means* include prayer, Bible study, fellowship, preaching, and communion. God

---

44. Cubie, *Into His Likeness: Various Papers on the Doctrine of Entire Sanctification*, 25.

45. Moore, Frank. *Coffee Shop Theology* (Kansas City: Beacon Hill Press, 1998), 88.

46. Wesley, J. Eby, Lyons, George, and Truesdale, Al. *A Dictionary of the Bible and Christian Doctrine in Everyday Language* (Kansas City: Beacon Hill Press of Kansas City, 2004), 181.

uses these *means* to draw us closer to Him and experience His grace in our lives. Wesley said that humans are the only beings that are "capable of God."[47] That is to say, we are created in the image of the Creator, but we are also created in a way that is able to receive grace from God. Not only do we bear the image of God, but we also carry with us a capacity to receive God if we choose to respond. The New Testament affirms our ability to choose and the inheritance we will receive as co-heirs with Christ when we become children of God. Through the "means of grace" we encounter the presence of God. In turn, we can reflect His presence (image) in our daily lives.

The Imago Dei in Today's World

Imago dei was something I learned about in my religion classes at college. To understand this doctrine is to discover meaning and worth, purpose, and direction. The doctrine has been neglected or not as emphasized as much as other beliefs. Nevertheless, the importance of this doctrine lies in God's desire to transform us from the inside out. Understanding who we are in Christ, and who we are to become through sanctifying grace, is a journey in freedom and purpose. The image of God can and will be restored in us.

The *imago dei* is more than a theological term. It is something we can discover in us as we grow in relationship to Christ. Christians often lose sight of this important process after they first become a follower of Jesus Christ. Many focus on "getting to heaven" (which is vital and necessary), which overshadows the equally important growth in grace. The finish is just as important as the start in our journey with God. Re-imagining who you are and who you've been created to be will free you from the world's ideals and allow you to live in fearless trust and wild abandon to God's Kingdom and call. With the coming of Christ and the image being restored in His person and in His deity, we find a new reason to dwell on this doctrine. We find a new reason to seek out God's divine stamp on our hearts and discover its potential to draw us further into grace.

---

47. Dunning, H. Ray. *Grace, Faith, and Holiness* (Kansas City: Beacon Hill of Kansas City, 1988), 159.

How can we discover the *imago dei* in us? How can it become a sacred rule of life? Let's explore ways you can become more aware of the *imago dei*.

Check your spiritual temperature and determine whose image you are living in.

How mindful are you of the fact that you have been created in the image of God? A way to become more mindful of this truth is by setting reminders for yourself, or "checking your temperature." When you wake up in the morning do you seek to live by God's ways or your own? Ask yourself in a journal or have an accountability friend who will ask you about whose image you are living in. Are you trying to live as a reflection of the world or in the image of God? Do you spend time with Christ in your mind, devotion, or in service? Do you allow God to work in you and through you? Have you taken every thought captive, making it obedient to Christ? These are all questions that will help you gauge your spiritual temperature.

"We demolish arguments and every pretension that sets itself up against the knowledge of God, and we take captive every thought to make it obedient to Christ" (2 Corinthians 10:5, TNIV).

Start something new.

The Bible tells us that we have become a new creation in Christ; the old things have passed away. Spend a moment during the week seeking new ways God is at work in your life. It's so easy to get caught up in the schedule and monotony, and live without challenge or passion. God has worked salvation in your life; ask God how you can sing a new song (Psalms 98:1) for the marvelous things that have been done. For some, it may be discovering a way to reach out to others through a youth group program, outreach service, volunteering, or helping someone who isn't popular or loved. You may have a gift that God has given you, but you are afraid of letting others know about it. Maybe you can sing, create, dance, or do graphic design. Whatever it is, uncover the thing that you are afraid of unleashing a little at a time to see how God can use your uniqueness to honor Him.

"For this reason I remind you to fan into flame the gift of God, which is in you" (2 Timothy 1:6a).

Celebrate Christmas a few times during the year.

Go to the dollar store and buy little gifts for those you love, cover your bedroom door in wrapping paper, and play Christmas carols. Go all out. Do this to remember the image that lives in each one of us through Jesus Christ. The Christmas season becomes an incredible way to remember how Jesus is Immanuel, God with us. Jesus brings the full restoration of the image into focus. His birth, life, and death point us to that image and give us an understanding of God.

"The virgin will conceive and give birth to a son, and they will call him Immanuel (which means 'God with us')" (Matthew 1:23, TNIV).

Exercise dominion.

There is a clear relationship between the "image" and the "dominion" that goes along with it. Be mindful of how your existence impacts creation. Help raise awareness by recycling, planting a garden, taking a walk on the beach, throwing away your trash, using less, buying less, and consuming less. There are all sorts of books and websites that can help you serve God and save the creation that was given to us to take care of. With dominion comes value and responsibility. Write down some ways you can give value to the things around you. What are your responsibilities to God's creation?

Live justly and practice compassion.

We live in a world that is quick to judge and quick to place labels. Think about your circles of influence, your friends and the people you communicate with on a regular basis. Who does your group tend to shut out? Whether your responses are intentional or not, who do you tend to neglect? Who do you make fun of? Who do you leave alone? Can you begin to develop ways of including others (even others who are different from you)? Can you begin to think in terms of God's image existing in every human being, no matter who they are or what they look like? Try to see God's image in those around you before you react. Ask for God to give you a heart of compassion and restraint for times when you are tempted to devalue, oppress, or take advantage of someone or something in creation.

"It is necessary to underscore that, no matter how one interprets the imago dei, the very presence of that image implies that every human being with whom we relate carries that image, and to devalue, oppress, or destroy a human being is to devalue, oppress or destroy the very image of God . . . it is important to note that in this text both the man and the woman have been created after the image and likeness of God, and that therefore the woman's dignity is the same as the man's."[48]

"So in Christ Jesus you are all children of God through faith, for all of you who were baptized into Christ have clothed yourselves with Christ. There is neither Jew nor Gentile, neither slave nor free, neither male nor female, for you are all one in Christ Jesus. If you belong to Christ, then you are Abraham's seed, and heirs according to the promise" (Galatians 3:26-29, TNIV).

Immerse yourself in the Bible.

Find a way that works for you to read, study, and meditate upon the written Word. The Bible is God's revelation to us and we can become more like Christ when we read it and allow the Holy Spirit to work in our lives. Developing spiritual disciplines, like reading God's Word, will help you see Christ more clearly and understand the image of God in you. One way of reading the Bible is through a practice called *lectio divina*, or divine reading (discussed in chapter 4). We gain access to the infinite reservoir of God's love and forgiveness when we seek God daily through spiritual habits. A great book to help you learn the habit of *lectio divina* is called *Enjoy the Silence* by Duffy and Maggie Robbins. They note the four steps of *lectio divina*:

"A French Benedictine monk named Dom Marimion describes lectio divina in terms of fours steps: "We read (lectio) under the eye of God (meditatio) until the heart is touched (oratio) and leaps into flame (contemplatio)."[49]

Finding a way to let the Word of God breathe in you will help restore the image of God in you and help you to see it more in others.

---

48. Gonzales, Justo. Perez, Zaida. *An Introduction to Christian Theology* (Nashville: Abingdon, 2002), 66-67.

49. Robins, Duffy and Maggie. *Enjoy the Silence* (Grand Rapids: Invert/Zondervan, 2005), 15.

Live in freedom from bondage.

"The restoration to the image of God to a true expression of dominion begins with a deliverance from bondage. Christ came 'to deliver all those who through fear of death have been in lifelong bondage'" (Heb. 2:15).[50]

Perhaps this is the first thing we should do to begin to understand the image of God in us.

Jesus tells us to ask and we shall receive, seek and we will find, knock and the door will be opened to us. God is able to break apart anything that hinders us or entangles us in our spiritual journey. Pray for God to break the bondage of sin in your life. Pray for God's sanctifying work to make you holy and free from willful sin. Living in bondage keeps us from seeing ourselves as we were meant to be.

"Therefore, since we are surrounded by such a great cloud of witnesses, let us throw off everything that hinders and the sin that so easily entangles. And let us run with perseverance the race marked out for us" (Hebrews 12:1, TNIV)

Final Thoughts

The image of God is in you and in every person who has been created. It has potential to reshape our dreams and give us hope for the future. May you uncover this sacred image and trust in Jesus to guide you in grace.

---

50. Cubie, p. 25.